APOLLO 8

APOLLO 8

The Mission That Changed Everything

MARTIN W. SANDLER

CANDLEWICK PRESS

First edition 2018

Library of Congress Catalog Card Number pending
ISBN 978-0-7636-9489-0

18 19 20 21 22 23 LEO 10 9 8 7 6 5 4 3 2 1

Printed in Heshan, Guangdong, China

This book was typeset in Adobe Garamond Pro.

Candlewick Press
99 Dover Street
Somerville, Massachusetts 02144

visit us at www.candlewick.com

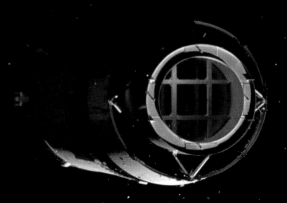

For Mimi and Roger Hewlitt
and Betsey and Peter Nelson
Friends Forever

CONTENTS

PROLOGUE

THE YOUNGEST MAN ever elected president of the United States stood before Congress. It was May 25, 1961, and John F. Kennedy was about to make one of the boldest, most surprising, most audacious speeches an American president had ever made. "I believe," he declared, "that this nation should commit itself to achieving the goal, before this decade is out, of landing a man on the moon and returning him safely to the Earth. No single space project in this period will be more impressive to mankind, or more important for the long-range exploration of space; and none will be so difficult or expensive to accomplish. . . . In a very real sense, it will not be one man going to the moon . . . it will be an entire nation. For all of us must work to put him there."

President John F. Kennedy inspired the nation in many ways—including when he challenged the United States to put a human on the moon before the end of the 1960s.

Once the members of Congress got over their shock, they broke into thunderous applause. The country was in the midst of one of the most tumultuous and frightening periods in world history. Since 1948, the United States and the communist Soviet Union had been engaged in the so-called Cold War. It was a bitter confrontation, driven by each side's desire to spread its ideology, power, and spheres of influence throughout the world, marked in particular by the tensions caused by the conflict between Russian expansion versus the determination of the United States to halt the spread of communism.

It was a struggle that by May 1961 had already seen the world's two great superpowers come close to outright war on more than one occasion. In their intense rivalry, the United States and the Soviet Union weren't competing just for political control on Earth. Another conflict lay at the heart of the Cold War: a race to dominate space. It would become the most fiercely contested race in history. And, when President Kennedy made his declaration to Congress, the United States was losing badly.

The space race had begun on October 5, 1957, when Americans awoke to the startling news that the Soviet Union had launched the world's first artificial satellite. Called Sputnik 1, it was circling the Earth every ninety-eight minutes at eighteen thousand miles per hour. It was an unprecedented development, but in the midst of the Cold War, it was not only shocking; it also struck terror and panic into the hearts and minds of millions across the United States.

Sputnik 1 was all anyone could talk about. Two of the nation's leading newspapers, the *New York Times* and the *Washington Post,* gave the news larger headlines than almost any in their long histories. *Newsweek* magazine scrapped its freshly printed issue, discarding more than a million copies featuring a cover story about Detroit's new line of cars. The replacement *Newsweek* cover showed an artist's interpretation of Sputnik. Inside, headlines included "The Red Conquest" and "Why We're Lagging." That week's *Life* magazine had an even more ominous take: "The Case for Being Panicky."

The Soviet satellite Sputnik 1 launched the world
into the space age and gave Russia an early lead
in what became a highly pressured space race
with the United States.

Sputnik 1 was a tremendous Cold War setback for America. "In the eyes of the world," stated U.S. vice president Lyndon B. Johnson, "first in space means first, period; second in space is second in everything." As Sputnik 1 circled overhead, Soviet head of state Nikita Khrushchev boasted that "People of the whole world are pointing to this satellite. They are saying the United States has been beaten." Many Americans began to wonder if he was right. And there was something more: both government officials and private citizens were worried that if the Russians could place a satellite high over the Earth, then they might also be able to fire missiles from space. The United States, declared the *New York Times,* was in not only a space race but also a race for survival. In 1958, the United States government, desperate to win this race, established a new agency, the National Aeronautics and Space Administration (NASA), to run its space program.

But the situation only got worse. On April 12, 1961, Russian cosmonaut Yuri Gagarin became the first human to orbit the Earth. It was an extraordinary Russian triumph. In response to the Soviet success, the *New York Times* declared that "only Presidential emphasis and direction will chart an American pathway to the stars."

At the time, President Kennedy was embroiled in Cold War crises in almost every corner of the world. In Cuba, Russia had established a communist government only sixty miles from the United States; in Germany, Russian-backed communists had taken over half of the capital city of Berlin; and in Vietnam, a civil war threatened to spawn an even greater confrontation between the United States and the Soviet Union.

The *Times* was right: presidential leadership was needed for America to advance in the space race. Increasingly, President Kennedy began to ask his advisers, "How can we catch up? There is nothing more important."

Kennedy's extraordinary speech a month later was the first step. His dramatic call to put an American on the moon by the end of 1969 galvanized

NASA. Less than a month before his speech, NASA had launched astronaut Alan Shepard into space, but Shepard's suborbital flight paled in comparison to Russian accomplishments. Still, it was a beginning, and it gave Kennedy the confidence to reach for the moon.

Tragically, Kennedy would never live to see that extraordinary goal achieved. On November 22, 1963, he was assassinated while riding in a presidential motorcade in Dallas, Texas. After Kennedy's assassination, the goal he had set, to reach the moon, became more than just a rallying cry — it became a memorial. As the decade progressed, NASA carried out spaceflights that, despite continued Soviet successes, brought the United States neck and neck with Russia in the space race. In late December 1968, another American mission was about to lift off. Its name was Apollo 8.

Apollo 8 was different from the crewed spaceflights, American and Russian, that had gone before it. Not only was the flight to be launched by the largest, most powerful rocket ever built, but all previous missions had been either suborbital or Earth-orbiting. Now three astronauts — Frank Borman, Jim Lovell, and Bill Anders — were to attempt to become the first humans to break the bonds of Earth. Apollo 8 was headed for the moon.

A HISTORIC CHANGE IN PLANS

DECEMBER 21, 1968: launch day for Apollo 8.
Tens of thousands of spectators at the launch viewing sites
gazed at a gigantic rocket with a tiny space capsule perched
atop its peak.

A technician works atop the "white room," perched beside the top of the Saturn V rocket. The Apollo 8 astronauts entered their spacecraft through this special room.

The rocket was unlike anything the world had ever seen. Standing 363 feet tall—about the height of a thirty-six-story building—and weighing 6.2 million pounds, the Saturn V was truly amazing. Its five first-stage engines produced a combined thrust of 7.5 million pounds (about 160 million horsepower), more than seventy-five times the power of a 747 airliner taking off. The rocket was so powerful that in the first second of its firing, it burned nearly forty thousand pounds of fuel. When the first test was launched, the sound waves it produced were so strong that a full four miles away, at the launch viewing area, news anchors had to keep hold of their television booths to prevent them from collapsing around them.

"Everything about the Saturn V was bigger," stated NASA's director of launch operations Rocco Petrone. "If you had to pick up a valve, you couldn't pick it up by hand. You had to get a forklift truck." Most amazing of all was the building in which the rocket was assembled: it was, of necessity, such a mammoth structure (716 feet long, 518 feet wide, and 526 feet tall) that it actually had its own climate. Unless all the fans in the building were circulating the air inside, clouds, created by the enormous amount of warm, moist air trapped at the top of the structure, would form and it would rain.

Apollo 8's original mission was to test equipment, including a capsule called a lunar lander, which would allow astronauts on a later flight to land on the moon. However, as the time for launch approached, it became clear that problems in the construction of the lunar lander meant that it would not be ready in time for Apollo 8's scheduled liftoff. Disappointed NASA officials decided that preparations for a launch had gone too far to cancel the flight. Apollo 8 would be sent off with the primary goal of testing how Saturn V handled the launch of a crewed space capsule.

Then something totally unexpected happened. In August 1968, NASA officials received word from the Central Intelligence Agency (CIA) that a Soviet rocket capable of carrying two people to the moon—but not landing them

PIONEERS OF ROCKETRY

The Saturn rocket remains the tallest, heaviest, and most powerful rocket ever put into operation, but the development of rocketry itself dates as far back as the 1100s, when the Chinese began using rockets in warfare. The earliest practical work on rocket engines designed for spaceflight took place in the early 1900s, and three innovators—Konstantin Tsiolkovsky in Russia, Hermann Oberth in Germany, and Robert Goddard in the United States—are widely regarded as the pioneers of modern rocketry.

Tsiolkovsky (1857–1935), an obscure schoolteacher in a remote region of Russia, was inspired by the science fiction of Jules Verne and H. G. Wells. In 1903, he declared that rockets would be the best means of traveling into space and laid out many of the principles of modern spaceflight. Most important, he detailed how, because the pull of Earth's gravity is strongest near the surface, a huge amount of thrust is needed to launch a rocket into space, but once it gains enough speed and distance from Earth, the engine could be turned off and it—or the spacecraft it carried—would coast on its own. Tsiolkovsky was also the first to propose multi-stage rockets, each powered by its own engine or engines, to carry a spacecraft far out into space. He theorized that as each stage burns up its fuel, it can be jettisoned, making the spacecraft lighter and more efficient. Tsiolkovsky also noted that liquid, rather than solid, fuels would produce the most controllable combustion for rockets designed for space travel. Tsiolkovsky never experimented with rockets, but his theories profoundly influenced the rocketeers who followed him.

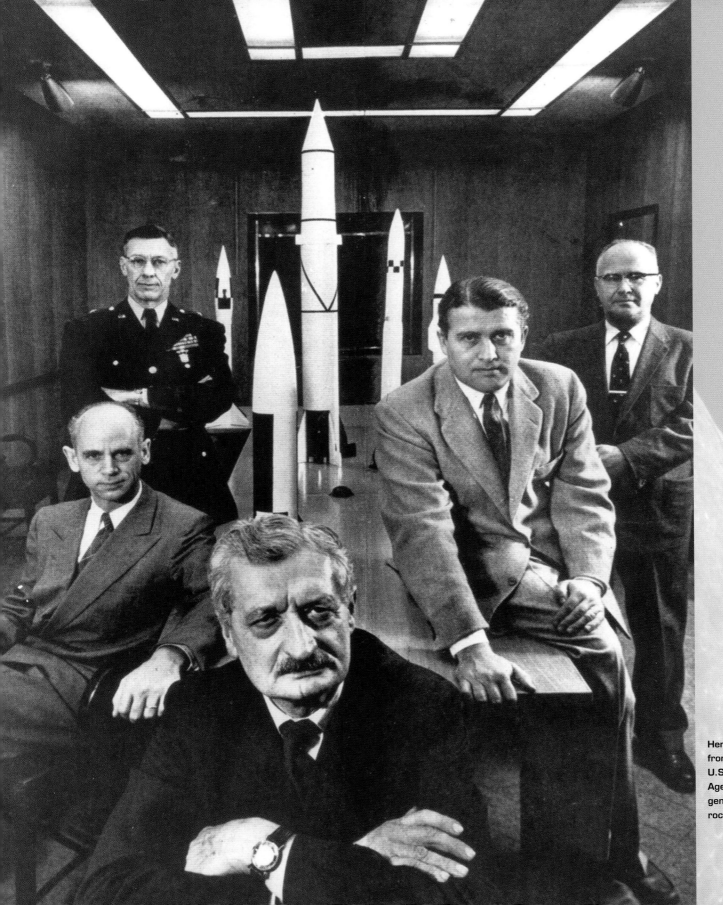

Hermann Oberth (center, front) with officials of the U.S. Army Ballistic Missile Agency. Oberth inspired generations of future rocket scientists.

The work and writings of German rocket scientist Hermann Oberth (1894–1989) largely echoed and reinforced those of Tsiolkovsky. Like his Russian counterpart, with whose work he was familiar, he was convinced that the key to space travel was multiple-stage rockets. "If there is a small rocket on top of a big one," he wrote, "and if the big one is jettisoned and the small one is ignited, then their speeds are added." Oberth experimented with several types of liquid fuel to achieve ever-higher speeds. Perhaps his greatest contribution was as a mentor to a young Wernher von Braun, the man destined to become the architect of the Saturn V.

Like Tsiolkovsky, American engineer and inventor Robert Goddard (1882–1945) fell in love with the idea of rocketry and space travel after reading the science fiction of Jules Verne. He was in high school when he declared, "It is difficult to say what is impossible, for the dream of yesterday is the hope of today and the reality of tomorrow." As a physics research fellow, Goddard obtained two patents for rocket propulsion, one for a multistage rocket and the other for a rocket using solid and liquid fuel. His work *A Method of Reaching Extreme Altitudes,* published in 1919 while he was a professor of physics at Clark University, became standard reading for all students of rocketry.

Over his lifetime, Goddard registered 214 patents for various rocket components. Perhaps his greatest contribution took place on March 16, 1926, near Auburn, Massachusetts, with the launch of a rocket that rose 184 feet in 2.5 seconds, an accomplishment widely regarded as the beginning of the modern age of rocketry and that set the stage for space travel. Eleven years later, Goddard launched a rocket that rose to an altitude of 8,900 feet. He was still experimenting with rockets and rocket engines when he died in August 1945.

Robert Goddard was one of the first to recognize that rockets could one day take humans to the moon. Here he poses with his first liquid-fueled rocket on the day of its launch.

Apollo 8

The Apollo 8 command
and service module being
hoisted high inside the
Vehicle Assembly Building,
where it will then be
attached to the three-stage
Saturn V rocket

on it—was being moved into launch position. It looked like the Soviets were about to outmaneuver the United States in space once again. "We learned . . . through our intelligence that the Soviet moon rocket was going to be tested with human beings" on board, Apollo director of flight operations Christopher Kraft recalled. "That would have been a devastating blow to our moon program because, even though the Soviets weren't going to land at that point, they would always be able to say that they had gotten there first."

George Low, manager of the Apollo Spacecraft Program, was determined to turn things around. "Low," said space historian Andrew Chaikin, "very quietly reviewed the situation and came up with this brilliant idea to take [Apollo 8] and instead of sending it into Earth orbit with a lunar lander that wasn't going to be ready, send it to the moon without a lander. Just do the part that says we're gonna go from the Earth to the moon, test out the communications, the navigation, all of those things that you're going to have to do anyway, later on for a landing. You don't need the Lunar Module for that mission."

It was an enormous gamble and Low knew it. But he also knew that if it worked, it would be a vital step toward President Kennedy's goal of landing a man on the moon before the decade was over, in just two more years. And reaching the moon before the Soviet Union would be a symbolic victory as well. As Chaikin put it, "NASA wanted to beat the Russians. That's what this program was about, to show the world that the American system, the American way of doing things, could do great things and that was as much a public relations goal as an engineering goal."

Low had to gain the approval and support of the head of the Apollo project, Christopher Kraft. Years later, Kraft recalled Low coming to him with his idea: "'Can we do a lunar fly-by? Can we fly around the moon and come back? Do you think that is possible to do?' And my first reaction to that was no, I don't think we can do it . . . to get all the control center ready, to get the network ready, to get the crews trained, to get ourselves, the flight control team, trained,

Flanked by Air Force Major General Vincent Huston and Manned Spacecraft Center director Robert Gilruth, Christopher Kraft and George Low—two of the people most responsible for sending Apollo 8 around the moon—study a screen in mission control.

and to be confident that we know what we are doing, I think it would be a very difficult thing to do."

There was another huge consideration for NASA to take into account. Low's plan was risky not only for the astronauts who would be making the flight but also for those sending them off. "For the people on the ground," stated astronaut Walter Cunningham, "it was a big step for them. Making life-and-death decisions about somebody else's life is a lot more difficult than making one about your own."

George Low was well aware of what he would be asking astronauts Frank Borman, Jim Lovell, and Bill Anders to do. Although all three men had been both fighter pilots and test pilots and were accustomed to facing huge challenges, neither Low nor Chris Kraft was certain that they would willingly take on risks greater than they could have imagined. They needn't have worried. All three astronauts readily agreed to carry out the revised mission.

Borman agreed immediately, saying that he was in the space program to beat the Russians both in the space race and the Cold War. Lovell also agreed without hesitation. As the spacecraft's command module pilot, he would be the flight's navigator, charting a path no one had ever traveled before. "I was ecstatic," he stated. "For me, the idea of going to explore a new planet far outweighed the fear of something going wrong." As for Bill Anders, arguably the most adventurous of the three men, he had waited for five years after completing NASA's astronaut training to fly into space. He was not about to say no to the greatest space adventure yet.

One huge hurdle remained. Apollo 8's mission plan could not be changed without the approval of NASA's top official, Administrator James E. Webb. Haunted by the memory of a tragic fire that had taken the lives of Apollo 1's three astronauts and all too aware that no human cargo had ever been launched by a Saturn V rocket, Webb's first reaction was far from positive. It was, in fact, a loud "Are you out of your *mind*?" But Low, having already convinced Kraft,

SERGEI KOROLEV

One of the greatest differences between the American and the Russian space programs was that the United States kept almost nothing about its operations, even its failures, a secret, while Russia kept much of its space program, particularly its failures, hidden. The greatest Russian space secret was the man responsible for Sputniks 1, 2, and 3, as well as the spacecraft that carried Yuri Gagarin into Earth orbit and other engineering feats: Sergei Korolev. Fearful that a man of such importance, responsible for much of the Soviets' gigantic lead in the space race, would be a target for assassination by the United States, the Russian government kept his very existence a secret.

Two of the great heroes of the Soviet space program: Yuri Gagarin and Sergei Korolev

Korolev was born in Zhitomir, Russia, in 1906. At age eighteen, Korolev, who had been interested in aviation since childhood, was admitted to the Kiev Polytechnic Institute. He spent two years there, during which he designed his first aircraft, but he then transferred to the leading engineering school in Russia, where he earned an aeronautical degree and, just as important, became a protégé of Andrei Tupolev, one of the most renowned aircraft designers in the world.

In 1931, Korolev and a colleague founded the Moscow rocketry association GIRD (Group for Investigation of Reactive Movement). Two years later, he directed the testing of Russia's first liquid-fuel rocket and assisted with its launch. In 1936, he designed the Soviet Union's first rocket-propelled aircraft. Then the Russian army, aware of the military potential of rockets, drafted Korolev into a government-run research program.

The 1920s and 1930s were a terrible time in the history of Russia. The Soviet Union was ruled by Joseph Stalin, one of the most evil men in history. Although figures vary widely, it is indisputable that as dictator, Stalin had at least three million people put to death. Some historians believe the number was closer to sixty million. Stalin also sent millions of people to prison or sentenced them to work in brutal conditions in mines at the far reaches of the Soviet empire. Most of these death or prison sentences were handed down for no apparent reason and were simply the result of Stalin's mood.

In June 1938, despite all that he had already achieved for Russia, Sergei Korolev became one of Stalin's victims. Arrested on false charges, he spent months doing hard labor on a railroad before being sent to prison and then to Siberia to work night and day in a gold mine deep underground.

Six years later, Korolev's fortunes suddenly changed again. Recognizing Korolev's skill and knowledge, Stalin ordered Korolev's release from custody and appointed him chief designer of Soviet rocketry with the expectation that he would contribute greatly to the war with Nazi Germany. During his years in prison, Korolev had lost all his teeth, had his jaw broken, and suffered a heart attack. But despite the treatment he'd received at the hands of his country, he dreamed of Soviet dominance in space and began to develop the world's first intercontinental ballistic missile—a missile that achieved spaceflight on its way to its target. By 1954, with the government's blessing, he started to develop the technology and the equipment that would lead to Sputnik 1. In 1957, he confided to his wife that "In every century, men were looking at the dark blue sky and dreaming. And now I'm very close to the greatest dream of mankind."

Korolev was working on a Soviet counterpart to the Saturn V rocket when he was admitted to a hospital with ailments that had originated with the physical abuse he had suffered in prison. On January 14, 1966, the man who had launched the world into the space age by designing, building, and launching Sputnik 1 died on the operating table. He was fifty-nine years old.

The greatest Russian space secret came to light later that day. The state-run newspaper *Pravda* ran a lengthy obituary, and for the first time, Russians learned what a hero Sergei Korolev was. To this day, scores of space experts and historians, Russian and American, believe that the loss of this Soviet visionary cost Russia the race to achieve crewed lunar orbit and then to land a human on the moon.

was able to persuade Webb to give the go-ahead to the boldest venture not only in space exploration but in the history of exploration itself.

Few outside the NASA community had any doubts that the revised Apollo 8 mission was the most daring endeavor ever undertaken. And most also had no doubt that the spacecraft would leave Earth at one of the most troubling times in the nation's history.

Throughout 1968, the United States and its people had suffered one enormous shock after another, many of them the result of developments in the Southeast Asian nation of Vietnam. In 1954, the Vietnamese peninsula had been divided, with a communist regime in the North and a democratic government in the South. In 1959, North Vietnamese forces, with the goal of reuniting the country under communist rule and the backing of the Soviet Union, began a campaign of guerrilla warfare against the South. Fearing that a communist takeover of South Vietnam would lead to other communist takeovers in the region, the United States entered the conflict, sending first advisers and then, beginning in 1965, tens of thousands of ground troops to support democratic South Vietnam. It quickly became the most unpopular war in United States history.

In January 1968, North Vietnamese forces launched a massive campaign called the Tet Offensive with attacks on cities throughout South Vietnam. Close to four thousand American soldiers died in the Tet campaign, prolonging the divisive war and contributing to more and more protests in the United States.

On April 4, three months after the Tet Offensive, the nation's leading civil rights advocate, Dr. Martin Luther King Jr., was fatally shot in Memphis, Tennessee. King, a leader in the civil rights movement since the 1950s and particularly famous for his 1963 "I Have a Dream" speech, was in Memphis to support a sanitation workers' strike and was killed by a single rifle shot fired by James Earl Ray, an escapee from a Missouri prison.

U.S. soldiers in Vietnam faced guerrilla fighters in challenging terrain. Here, members of a U.S. marine regiment slog hip-high through water on their way to join up with their battalion.

King's assassination led to an outpouring of anger among African Americans and some of the most devastating race riots the nation had ever witnessed. Cities throughout the United States were rocked by major fires, looting, injuries, and the destruction of tens of millions of dollars' worth of property.

Only two months after King's assassination and less than five years after President Kennedy's, another devastating assassination shocked the nation. On June 5, 1968, Robert F. Kennedy, who had served in his brother John's cabinet as attorney general and who later had become a senator for New York, was fatally shot in a Los Angeles hotel.

The younger Kennedy, a champion of economic and racial justice, had emerged as the Democratic Party's leading candidate for president after Lyndon B. Johnson announced that he would not seek reelection. Johnson's approval rating had plummeted because of his aggressive Vietnam War policies. That night in June, when it became clear that he had won the critical California Democratic Party primary, Kennedy delivered a victory speech to almost two thousand supporters in the hotel ballroom. His speech delivered, Kennedy, surrounded by key supporters, left the ballroom to meet with the press elsewhere in the hotel. Taking a shortcut, aides led him into one of the hotel's kitchens, where, suddenly, a twenty-four-year-old Palestinian, convinced that Kennedy was anti-Palestinian, stepped out of the crowd and shot him three times with a pistol concealed inside a rolled-up campaign poster. Twenty-six hours later, Robert Kennedy died from his wounds at the age of forty-two.

It was almost too much for the country to bear. Two assassinations of two great national figures, each idolized by millions of people, had occurred within two months. All the while, the increasingly unpopular Vietnam War raged on and civil rights protests and antiwar protests continued unabated.

Yet one of the most shocking events of the year was still to come. In August, the Democratic Party held its national convention in Chicago. Sentiment against the Vietnam War had grown so heated that protesters had succeeded in closing down Columbia University in New York City. Now demonstrators flocked to Chicago, intent on pressuring the Democratic Party to turn against the war.

As the demonstrators, mostly young people, poured into the city, Chicago mayor Richard Daley ordered his police to do whatever they felt necessary to keep the protesters away from the convention site. For five days, thousands of protesters clashed with 11,900 Chicago police, 7,500 army troops, and 7,500 Illinois National Guardsmen. As protesters chanted "The whole world is watching," and a stunned nation *did* look on via television, police bloodied demonstrators with clubs and released tear gas into the streets. By the time the convention ended, 589 protesters had been arrested and more than 220 demonstrators and police officers had been injured.

Shock from the convention, despair over the violent deaths of Dr. Martin Luther King Jr. and Robert Kennedy, and anger and frustration over the Vietnam War continued to reverberate as December 21, the day of the Apollo 8 launch, drew closer. One thing was clear: the nation needed something good to happen.

AGAINST
ALL ODDS

ORDINARILY, it took months to create a flight plan for a venture into space. But amazingly, the flight plan for the first crewed mission to the moon was created in one long August-afternoon meeting in the flight director's office among the spacecraft's commander Frank Borman, NASA's highly experienced mission planner Bill Tindall, and several of flight director Christopher Kraft's best engineers and spaceflight experts. Part of the reason for such haste was the all-encompassing desire to beat the Russians to the moon, but there was also the understanding that four months was an incredibly short time in which to train three astronauts for all the tasks and procedures necessary for their unprecedented journey.

The Apollo 8 crew (left to right: Frank Borman, Jim Lovell, Bill Anders), dressed in casual attire, poses in front of the Saturn V rocket as it is about to be moved from the Vehicle Assembly Building to the launching pad.

As was the case in all of NASA's spaceflights, the three men selected to form Apollo 8's crew had been specially chosen. The flight's navigator, Jim Lovell, was the world's most experienced astronaut. Apollo 8 was Lovell's third space mission and he'd already spent more than 425 hours in space.

As a child, Lovell had had two great passions. Astronomy inspired him to spend hours studying the stars and the constellations, and rocketry led him to spend just as many hours drawing rockets of his own design. He even wrote to the American Rocket Society seeking information on how he could become a rocket engineer.

A graduate of the United States Naval Academy and a naval aviator with more than five thousand hours of flying time logged, at the age of thirty-four, Lovell was one of the nine men selected for astronaut training in 1962. A year after he spent 330 hours and 35 minutes in space with Frank Borman on Gemini 7, Lovell commanded the final Gemini mission, Gemini 12, during which pilot Edwin "Buzz" Aldrin performed three space walks.

The Gemini era gave way to Apollo, and Lovell's Apollo 8 responsibilities were particularly critical: to conduct all navigation during the farthest journey—by far—that any human had ever undertaken. And it was his responsibility to fire the special engines that permitted critical maneuvers such as propelling the spacecraft from Earth's orbit and heading it toward the moon, putting the craft into orbit around the moon, and, finally, releasing Apollo 8 from lunar orbit and heading it back toward Earth.

"We shifted into high gear in our training," Jim Lovell explained. "Space navigation was a new field for me. In Gemini elaborate navigation had never been necessary. Our earth orbits were always well defined by [mission control], and navigation was minimal. In Apollo it is much more sophisticated. The objective is to come very close to the moon but not hit it; then to make a return to earth on a very precise path. Translunar flight involves a long trajectory, and any small disturbance or error is multiplied by the distance. Thus these flights require constant navigational updates."

The least experienced member of the crew was thirty-five-year-old air force major William "Bill" Anders. A member of a family with a proud navy tradition (his father had been awarded the Navy Cross for his heroic actions in China during a Japanese attack on the American patrol boat to which he had been assigned), Anders had been selected to be an astronaut in 1963 after graduating from the United States Naval Academy and serving as a fighter pilot in the United States Air Force. Anders had been a member of the backup crew for the Gemini 11 mission but was still a space rookie when Apollo 8 launched.

Anders had his own motivation for taking part in Apollo 8: he was about to become the first scientist to fly in space. With advanced degrees in nuclear sciences as well as engineering, he was particularly interested in uncovering age-old secrets about the moon's composition and how the lunar surface was formed. Science and flight all fit into his greatest love—his passion for exploration. In Apollo 8, Bill Anders saw his chance to become one of the greatest explorers of all time.

In order to attempt this, Anders was required to make an enormous training adjustment. "I spent eighteen months training to fly the lunar module," he later explained. "What does a lunar module pilot do without a lunar module? I found out in a hurry. My new job was to learn the command and service modules inside out. I was responsible for the electrical power, environmental control, communications and propulsions systems—to make them behave properly during the flight and to be ready for any malfunction." Anders's changed responsibilities also included surveying the lunar surface for future landing sites and taking close-up pictures of the moon.

Forty-year-old air force colonel Frank Borman, the commander of the flight, was born in Gary, Indiana, in 1928. He developed serious sinus problems as a child, prompting his family to move to Tucson, Arizona, in search of a more healthful climate. Young Frank had already developed a love of everything

Lovell, Anders, and Borman suited up

related to flying, and the wide-open Arizona desert proved to be a perfect place for him and his father to test model airplanes. Borman was only fifteen years old when he got his pilot's license. By the time he was a senior in high school, he was absolutely certain that he wanted to spend his life flying airplanes.

In 1947, Borman entered the United States Military Academy and then the air force, where his assignments included fighter pilot, test pilot, and assistant professor at the Military Academy. In September 1962 he was one of nine men out of 253 applicants to be selected to become part of America's second group of astronauts.

By the time Apollo 8 launched, Borman was not a newcomer to space. In December 1965, he and fellow astronaut Jim Lovell had spent a record-setting fourteen days in Earth orbit aboard Gemini 7, a spacecraft smaller than an average bathroom stall. Gemini 7 proved that humans could withstand a space mission that lasted for at least two weeks and that astronauts could rendezvous with another spacecraft while in space, both necessary capabilities for landing astronauts on the moon and bringing them safely back to Earth.

With Apollo 8, Frank Borman was a man on a very deeply felt personal mission. In 1949, while at the Military Academy, he was one of twelve cadets chosen to tour Europe. There, he witnessed the beginnings of the Cold War firsthand. Seeing communist oppression spreading and millions of people losing their freedom had a profound impact on Borman and sparked his desire to be an astronaut. "I didn't go into the NASA program to pick up [moon] rocks," he would later proclaim. He became an astronaut because he saw himself as a Cold War warrior and regarded the space race as the most important battle he could fight. And he was convinced that nothing would do more to bring about victory than the success of Apollo 8.

Now, as he was about to embark on the most important undertaking of his life, Frank Borman was defined by his confidence. He knew he could make the right onboard flight decisions and get his crew to carry them out. Nothing mattered more than getting his spacecraft to the moon, becoming the first humans to circle it, and getting himself and Lovell and Anders back home safely. To Borman, anything else was an unnecessary, and potentially damaging, distraction. When NASA officials proposed that Apollo 8 orbit the moon some twenty or thirty times, Borman rejected the idea, telling them that ten orbits was quite enough and anything more ambitious only increased the chances of something going wrong. When a senior NASA officer suggested that one of the astronauts perform a space walk on their way to the moon, Borman refused to even consider it. "What's the main objective?" he explained later. "The main objective was to go to the Moon, do enough orbits so that [we could] be pathfinders for [a moon landing] and get . . . home. Why complicate it?"

It was a hard-nosed, eyes-on-the-prize approach that won Borman the respect of his fellow astronauts but did not make it easy for them. "I don't know that I could spend a month on a desert island with Frank," Anders would say halfway into the mission. "We might tear each other apart before it was over. I might get two weeks in with Lovell, though."

As Apollo 8's commander, Frank Borman was put through the most varied and intense four-month training of all. Commanding a spacecraft flying to the moon, around it, and then returning to Earth meant becoming totally familiar with the workings of every switch, readout, and control on the spacecraft's instrument panel. It meant hours spent in the most important of all the training devices: the flight simulator.

The flight simulator contained exact replicas of every piece of equipment and every instrument that the astronauts would interact with inside Apollo 8. Seated at consoles outside the simulator were special instructors whose job it was to create malfunctions in the astronauts' practice flights and to give them vital training in responding quickly and correctly to each potentially fatal error.

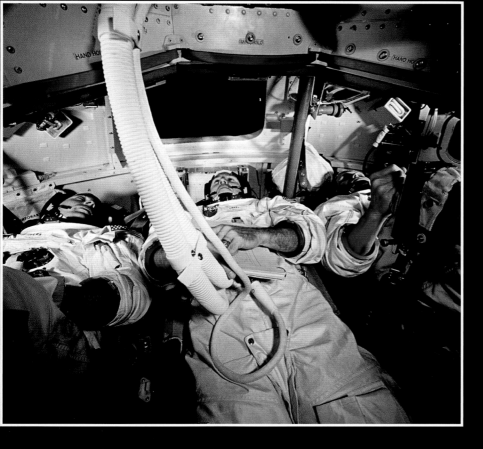

Far left: The Apollo 8 astronauts in front of the flight simulator

Top left: The astronauts practicing for launch

Top right: Borman leaving the flight simulator

Left: The astronauts practicing for splashdown

And for all three men, the training routine meant becoming as familiar as possible with the spacecraft's onboard computer. Although it was primitive when compared to today's desktop computers (it had only 33,000 words of memory), it was an unusual, revolutionary piece of technology and was essential in calculating the spacecraft's position and in setting its path to the moon and back.

When their accelerated training was over, Borman, Lovell, and Anders were as familiar as possible with the workings of the Apollo 8 spacecraft and with the lunar landscape to which they were headed. They were, they believed, as ready for the mission as they were ever going to be.

At 2:30 in the morning on December 21, Deke Slayton, one of the Mercury Seven astronauts—those Americans who went into space as part of America's first crewed missions—and now NASA's director of flight crew operations,

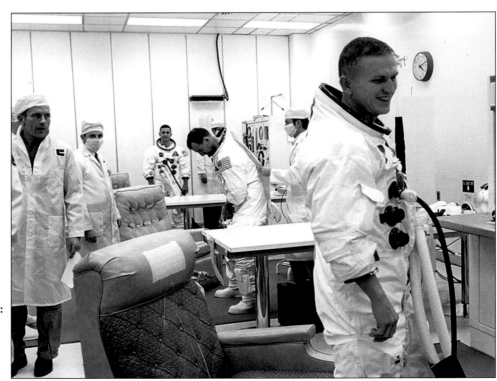

The Apollo 8 astronauts rehearse one of their most critical preflight procedures: making certain that their space suits and the equipment attached to them are in perfect working order.

woke Borman, Lovell, and Anders. According to the latest forecasts, the weather for the 7:51 a.m. launch was going to be excellent.

After completing a final medical examination, the astronauts sat down to the traditional flight crew's prelaunch breakfast of steak and eggs. Then they moved on to the suiting room, where technicians helped them into their spacesuits, rubber pressure gloves, and helmets. Carrying portable oxygen units, they left the Flight Crew Training Building and boarded a specially equipped transfer van for the eight-mile ride to Pad 39A.

Led by flight commander Frank Borman, the Apollo 8 crew leaves the suiting room. They will then enter the van that will take them to the launching pad.

They had spent months preparing for these moments. The sight of Saturn V was certainly not new to them, but as they approached the launchpad, they became filled with emotion. "The Saturn V was such an enormous machine," Borman later said. "And the size of the engines?! . . . It was an enormous thing. And I think I felt that more going up the morning of the launch. Because it was so quiet, nobody around it. . . . I don't want to say awe, a combination of admiration—yeah, maybe awe. Wonderment."

Careful of their life-preserving suits, the astronauts climbed out of the transfer van and into the service tower perched next to the rocket, where a small elevator took them 320 feet into the air. They stopped directly beside the spacecraft that would, they hoped, take them to the moon. First Borman, then Anders, and finally Lovell climbed into Apollo 8 and settled into their seats as comfortably as they could as the closeout crew hooked them up to oxygen hoses and communications lines.

It was an extraordinary opportunity for all three men, but it was as risky an endeavor as any adventurers had faced and many space experts gave it very little chance of succeeding. Even NASA flight director Gene Kranz had serious doubts about what the astronauts and the flight controllers were being asked to do. They would, he explained, be "threading the needle, shooting a spacecraft from a rotating Earth at the leading edge of the Moon, a moving target a quarter of a million miles away."

The enormous distance presented a particular risk. "This," stated the *Washington Post,* "will be the first flight in which troubled astronauts cannot return to earth in less than three hours. . . . An emergency trip home from the moon would take nearly three painful days."

Apollo 8 was the riskiest mission yet—some even said it was doomed. All the way to the moon and back, Borman, Lovell, and Anders would be making vital maneuvers. Some would require them to fire special engines for specific durations at specific times. The tiniest error could result in the astronauts being trapped in space forever.

The Saturn V was not only the largest and most powerful rocket ever built; it was also the most complex and most prone to disaster. Together, the Saturn V and the Apollo 8 spacecraft had 5.6 million parts. Even if 99.9 percent of these parts worked perfectly, that left 5,600 of them to cause a calamity. The Saturn V had only been tested twice, and both of these tests had been hampered by serious problems. The Saturn V had never before been used to carry humans into space. As Bill Anders later recalled, "During our preflight training, the other members of the crew often referred to me as the 'rookie.' I didn't particularly enjoy this bit of gamesmanship, but it was true that this was my first space flight. On the other hand, one wonders if everyone isn't a rookie when it comes to flying the first manned Saturn V on the first lunar flight."

For many NASA officials, none of these enormous dangers represented the greatest risk. Apollo 8 was being sent to the moon without a lunar landing module. A moon landing had never been part of Apollo 8's mission, but the lunar lander was designed to serve an additional purpose: if there was a serious problem with the command capsule, the lunar lander would serve as a lifeboat, one whose engines could get the astronauts safely home.

The astronauts were fully aware of the unprecedented risks and dangers they faced. In the days before launch, Frank Borman would step outside each evening and gaze up at the moon, seriously wondering if anyone could hit a target that far away. Flight director Gene Kranz confided to his closest friends that he believed the astronauts had a 50 percent chance of returning safely. Bill Anders did his own calculations. "I gave some thought to the odds," he would later say. "I figured we had a one-third chance of success, a one-third chance of a survivable accident and a one-third chance of not coming back." Jim Lovell, on the other hand, refused to calculate the odds. "If you worried about whether or not you were coming home," he claimed, "you wouldn't go in the first place."

AN EARLY DISASTER

All those connected with the space program were well aware of the enormous risks. Two years before the launch of Apollo 8, the space community received tragic proof of how real these dangers were.

In August 1966, the first Apollo command module had been delivered to NASA for testing leading up to the first crewed flight aimed at preparing for a moon landing. Three astronauts had been chosen: Edward H. White, Roger B. Chaffee, and the mission's captain, Virgil "Gus" Grissom. Forty-year-old Grissom was an air force lieutenant colonel who had already been into space as one of the Mercury Seven. Thirty-six-year-old White, also an air force lieutenant colonel, had trained with Borman and Anders and had been the first American to walk in space. Chaffee, a navy lieutenant commander, was the rookie of the group and was scheduled to make his first spaceflight six days after his thirty-second birthday.

The Apollo command module was extremely complex, and during its construction, some twenty thousand problems within its various complicated systems had to be corrected. Grissom, in particular, grew increasingly annoyed with the time it was taking to put the module into what he regarded as satisfactory condition.

On January 27, 1967, a full ground test was scheduled to check the flight's countdown procedures. The Apollo spacecraft was perched on top of the Saturn rocket with the three fully suited astronauts inside, positioned as they would be for their actual flight: Grissom in the command pilot's position on the left, White in the middle, and Chaffee on the right. As it would be for mission launch, the capsule's double-hulled hatch was tightly closed and the cabin was filled with pure oxygen.

A problem arose almost immediately after the astronauts entered the capsule at one p.m., when Grissom described a strange odor in his space suit. It was checked out, no problems were discovered, and the test continued for the next five hours, progressing with only a few annoying glitches. Then the communication system between the astronauts and those in flight central broke down.

Some of the engineers wanted to halt the test. Those in charge had barely announced their order to continue when they heard Gus Grissom shouting "Fire!" from inside the capsule. A second later, Roger Chaffee's voice rang out: "We've got a fire in the cockpit."

On their monitors, those overseeing the test witnessed the horrifying sight of flames leaping about inside the capsule with

The crew of the ill-fated Apollo 1. Left to right: Gus Grissom, Edward White, and Roger Chaffee

White desperately trying to open the hatch and Chaffee yelling into the microphone, "Get us out. We've got a bad fire. We're burning up!"

When the technicians working outside the capsule realized what was happening, several raced forward to try to open the hatch but were driven back by an explosion that blew a hole in the side of the spacecraft. Six minutes went by before the fire could be put out. The temperature inside the capsule had risen to as high as 2500°F. Grissom, White, and Chaffee had died of asphyxiation within a minute of the fire erupting.

Over the next few weeks, nearly two thousand investigators took the destroyed spacecraft apart. Finally, they determined that the fire had been started by an electrical spark from a bundle of frayed wires on the floor near Grissom. It had ignited the pure oxygen atmosphere in the capsule and turned into an inferno.

It was a terrible tragedy, cruelly ironic in that three heroic American astronauts had lost their lives not in space but on the ground. It was a major setback to the nation's space program with the space race at its peak. And it made future Apollo flights seem even riskier. But the quest for the conquest of space would go on, carried out by people who agreed with Gus Grissom himself: "If we die," he had stated, "we want people to accept it. We're in a risky business. . . . The conquest of space is worth the risk of life."

Borman's wife was the least confident of all. Susan Borman loved her husband dearly, and no one could be prouder of all he had done for his country. And she knew how important the Apollo 8 mission would be, if successful. "We knew that the Russians were hell bent to do the same thing and by golly we were going to get there first," she later said. "But I didn't really think they would get them back. I just didn't see how they could. Everything was for the first time. Everything."

At 5:34 a.m. on December 21, with the astronauts seated in the command module, technicians closed and locked the spacecraft's enormous hatch. It was two hours and seventeen seconds to launch, and as the darkness gave way to a bright dawn, Anders gazed out one of the capsule's windows and spotted something moving: a hornet hovering outside the spacecraft. "She's building a nest," he remembered thinking, "and did she pick the wrong place to build it!"

For the next two hours, the crew was kept busy checking their instruments and taking care of last-minute details for NASA's spacecraft test conductor Dick Proffitt's final status check. With forty-five seconds left in the countdown, Borman confirmed that Apollo 8 was ready for launch. The countdown moved to thirty seconds, twenty seconds, twelve, eleven, ten . . .

At nine seconds, the Saturn V's first-stage rockets ignited. Enormous clouds of smoke billowed out from the launch tower. For the next nine seconds, gigantic clamps held the rocket in place as the engines built up thrust. Then, precisely as planned, the clamps fell away and seven million pounds of rocket, spacecraft, and astronauts lifted off on the first crewed flight outside of Earth's orbit.

Sitting in the VIP stands, Susan Borman thought it was "awesome . . . like watching the Empire State Building taking off." Amazed, the legendary Charles Lindbergh—the first person to fly across the Atlantic alone—commented that in the first second of the flight, the Saturn V would burn "ten times more fuel than what I did all the way to Paris." His wife, the writer Anne Morrow Lindbergh, watching from three miles away, gave it a more poetic description.

The rocket rose "slowly, as in a dream, so slowly it seemed to hang suspended on the cloud of fire and smoke." Of the shattering noise, she wrote, "The Earth shakes, cars rattle, vibrations beat in the chest. A roll of thunder prolonged, prolonged, prolonged."

Veteran newsperson Walter Cronkite had witnessed every one of NASA's crewed liftoffs, but none affected him as profoundly as the launch of Apollo 8. "It was all there in our emotions as it took off," he later said. "It was a combination of concern for their safety and knowing that this was this great pioneering adventure. It was an event beyond all other events. . . . The hopes of America, the hopes of the world perhaps . . . rested on the success of that mission. This was man escaping his environment really, out to the very moon itself, knowing that the moon would never look the same again, that once man had been there and we'd known they'd been there and returned safely. Everything was there and it all rested in that spaceship."

December 21, 1968, 7:51 a.m. (EST): The Apollo 8 space vehicle is launched from Pad A, Launch Complex 39, Kennedy Space Center, near Cape Canaveral, Florida.

WERNHER VON BRAUN

Unlike the Russians, who kept Sergei Korolev's existence a secret, NASA officials were totally open about their space leaders, particularly Wernher von Braun.

The man responsible for the development of the Saturn V rocket was born in Wyrzysk, Poland, in 1912 but was raised and educated in Thuringia, Germany. Although he demonstrated a natural musical ability, two early influences steered him toward a very different career, to which he would devote his life. First, his mother gave him a telescope and he became fascinated with astronomy. Second, while attending boarding school, he acquired a copy of the book *By Rocket into Planetary Space* by rocketry pioneer Hermann Oberth, who would become a mentor to von Braun and whom he would later call "the guiding-star of my life."

Rocket pioneer Hermann Oberth (left) and Wernher von Braun (center) look on as NASA scientist Charles Lundquist discusses orbital trajectories.

In 1933, while von Braun was working on his doctorate degree, Adolf Hitler and the Nazi Party came into power in Germany. A Nazi military captain arranged for a research grant so that von Braun could complete his doctoral thesis, *Construction, Theoretical, and Experimental Solution to the Problem of the Liquid Propellant Rocket*. When World War II began, von Braun became the head of Germany's rocket development program and created a powerful new weapon, the V-2 rocket. In September 1944, Hitler ordered V-2 attacks against England in an attempt to force the British to surrender. More than five thousand V-2s were fired, mostly at London. More than 2,700 people were killed and nearly six thousand were injured.

The V-2 attacks did not force the courageous British people to surrender, and by the spring of 1945, the Allies—led by the United States, Russia, and Great Britain—were well on their way to defeating Germany. Rather than surrender to the Russians, who were closing in on the Peenemünde facility, where the rocketry team had developed the V-2, von Braun and forty members of his rocketry team fled west and surrendered to the American army. By this time, von Braun was regarded as the world's greatest rocket scientist, and he and his team were taken to the United States and put to work developing ballistic missiles.

In October 1957, the appearance of Sputnik gave von Braun the opportunity he had longed for. He had always been far more interested in rockets to take people to the moon than in rockets for military purposes. Transferred from the military to NASA, he quickly demonstrated that his skills and experience gave the United States its best chance of beating the Soviet Union in their intense space race. In 1960, von Braun became head of the Marshall Space Flight Center in Huntsville, Alabama, where he developed the Saturn V rocket.

The enormity of the
Saturn V is evident
in this photograph of
Wernher von Braun in
front of the rocket's
engines.

Von Braun won many honors for his achievements. But there is a dark underside to the story as well.

Ever since his surrender to the American army, there has been controversy over how involved von Braun was in the Nazi Party. Even more serious are allegations that he was well aware that tens of thousands of slave laborers from Nazi concentration camps worked on constructing the V-2 rockets. Beyond that are allegations that von Braun knew that thousands of these slave laborers died from brutal treatment.

Recent revelations underscore these allegations, indicating that von Braun not only knew but actively singled out individuals to be put into the camps to work on the V-2s.

We will probably never know the full extent of von Braun's involvement, but it certainly blackens our understanding of "the greatest rocket scientist in history." Whether he should be honored or vilified, without Wernher von Braun and his genius in developing the Saturn V, the United States would never have been the first to the moon.

Wernher von Braun poses in his office at the Marshall Space Flight Center. Behind him are models of various NASA rockets.

TO THE MOON

CONCEIVED AND DEVELOPED under the direction of Wernher von Braun and based on the principles first espoused by rocketry pioneers Konstantin Tsiolkovsky, Hermann Oberth, and Robert Goddard, the Saturn V's enormous main engines were designed to ignite in three distinct stages. For the first two minutes following liftoff, Apollo 8's five first-stage engines built up velocity, propelling the spacecraft to a speed of over six thousand miles per hour and an altitude of forty miles. Then, exactly on schedule, the first-stage engines blew away and the second-stage engines ignited.

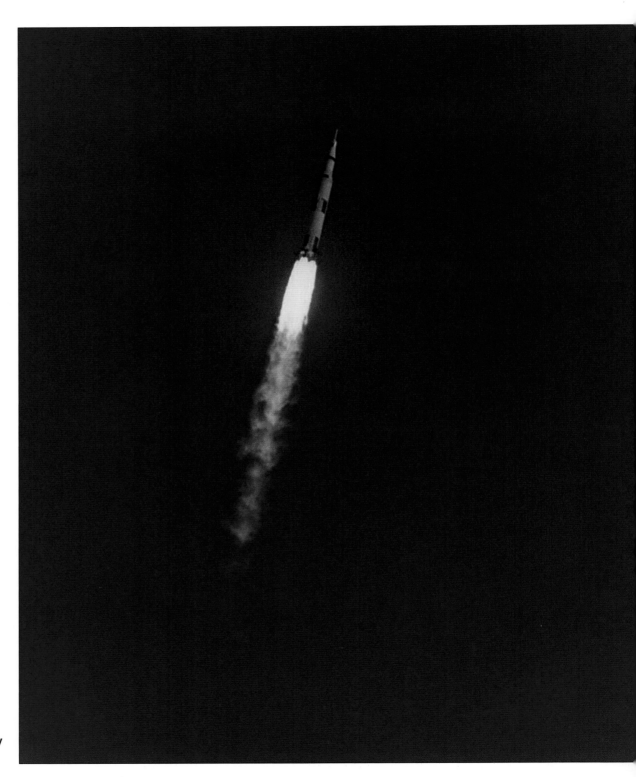

Apollo 8 climbs toward space and the moon after liftoff. Ahead lies a journey of some 250,000 miles.

With less weight, Saturn V built up even greater speed. In less than ten minutes, the rocket with its human cargo was one hundred miles over the Earth and the second-stage engines blew away.

The third-stage engine ignited and burned for the next two and a half minutes, driving the lighter-than-ever rocket and spacecraft higher and faster. Then, exactly eleven and a half minutes after launch, the third-stage engine cut off. This engine remained attached to the rocket. It would refire when the astronauts were ready to break out of Earth's orbit and head for the moon.

It was a flawless, albeit noisy and turbulent, launch. "There was a startling moment there," Anders recalled, "right at liftoff. Everybody got quite startled. Because we had simulated the hell out of everything—aborts and everything—but nobody had ever been on a Saturn V. . . . As we lifted off, you can imagine this rocket—it's a giant thing, but it's not bulky like an obelisk or like the Washington Monument; it's not rigid. It's more flexible. Not quite a whip antenna on your automobile, but somewhat like this. . . . So we were literally being thrown around. I mean, 'thrown around' is the best way I can describe it. I felt like a rat in the jaws of a giant terrier. I mean, here we'd hardly started, and already we had something that we hadn't simulated." Borman would recall how, as Saturn V burst through the sound barrier, he, Anders, and Lovell "were thrown forward against our straps and smashed back into the seat."

Anders, who had taken part in numerous mock launches in the simulators, was surprised at how much more turbulent the actual liftoff was. "Instinctively," he recounted, "I threw my hand up in front of my face. . . . Well, about the time I got my hand up here, the second stage cut in . . . and snapped my hand back into my helmet. And the wrist string around my glove made a gash across the helmet face plate. And then on we went. Well, I looked at that gash and I thought, 'Oh, my gosh, I'm going to get kidded for being the rookie on the flight' because, you know, I threw my hand up. Then I forgot about it. Well, after we were in orbit and the rest of the crew took their space suits off and cleaned their helmets, and I had gotten out of my seat and was stowing them, I noticed that both Jim and Frank had a gash across the front of their helmet. So, we were all rookies on that one."

Apollo 8 was now in Earth orbit, traveling at 17,400 miles per hour. For Bill Anders, the only one aboard who had never been in orbit, it was a special time. "After insertion into earth orbit," he later told an interviewer, "I had lots of tests to perform on the spacecraft systems, but like all rookies before me, I must confess to a sneak peek out the window every now and then. I was enthralled by the sights in earth orbit, by the waters, the islands, the continents. There was a large fire in Australia and lightning, a lot of it, over New Zealand. I wanted to see it all, but it had to be a brief look because we were on our way to the moon. It's too bad you can't stay in earth orbit for a day or so before you start on a lunar flight — just to get the benefit of the whole tour."

"In the early stages of the flight," Lovell recalled, "the thing that impressed me most was the sight of the earth receding. I could see all of Florida and the Cape, but I had seen that before. This time, as I watched, the entire east coast of the U.S. came into view, and the Caribbean, and Central America. I could see most of South America, almost to the South Pole. And there, as if I could put out my thumb and little finger to span the Atlantic Ocean, there was western Africa. All in one view. We were higher than man had ever been before."

Lovell could not resist radioing mission control and asking them to contact astronaut Pete Conrad, who had set the record for traveling the greatest distance from Earth two years before. On Gemini 11, he and Dick Gordon had reached a height of 850 miles, but now, "Tell Conrad," Lovell instructed, "he lost his record."

Even Borman, determined as he was to stay on top of his tasks and not get distracted by sight-seeing, could not resist the occasional glance out the window. Looking down to Earth, he delivered history's first weather forecast from space: "Tell the people in Tierra del Fuego to put on their raincoats," he radioed to mission control. "Looks like a storm is out there."

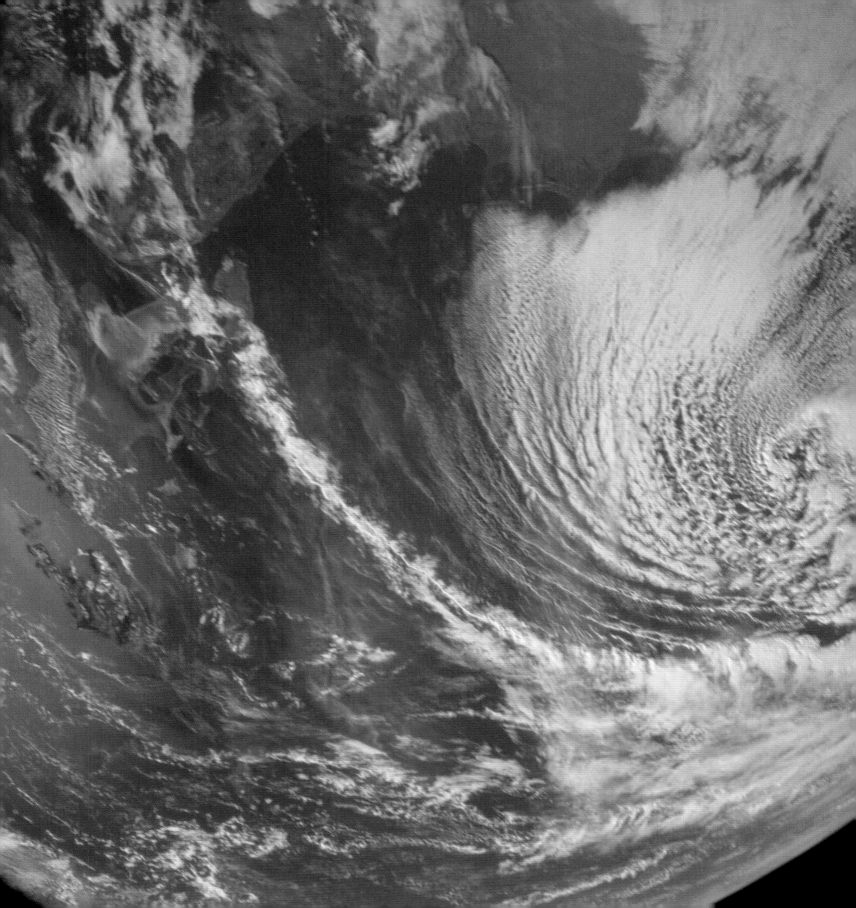

As former fighter and test pilots, Borman, Lovell, and Anders had experience watching the Earth recede as they gained altitude. But at this new height and unique view, it became an almost spiritual experience. "All of us had flown airplanes many times and seen airfields and buildings getting smaller as we climbed," Borman later wrote. "But now it was the whole globe receding in size, dwindling until it became a disk. We were the first humans to see the world in its majestic totality, an intensely emotional experience for each of us. We said nothing to each other, but I was sure our thoughts were identical — of our families on that spinning globe. And maybe we shared another thought I had. . . . *This must be what God sees.*"

The astronauts were now approaching one of the most critical steps of the entire mission, translunar injection, or TLI. It required refiring the third-stage Service Propulsion System, the SPS. If it was successful, Borman, Lovell, and Anders would be catapulted out of Earth orbit and into a 240,000-mile journey to the moon. If the engine failed to fire or if it fired inadequately, the historic mission would have to be aborted.

Before attempting TLI, Apollo 8 made three orbits around the Earth. During the second and third orbits, mission control, in Houston, Texas, and tracking stations around the world checked to make sure that all systems connected were operating properly. Astronaut Mike Collins and prime flight director Cliff Charlesworth were particularly busy. Collins's job was to stay in contact with Borman, Lovell, and Anders and relay any information to them that NASA felt they needed to know. Seated next to Collins at mission control, Charlesworth had the vital responsibility of making all final decisions regarding the mission. As soon as Apollo 8 entered its second Earth orbit, he checked in with dozens of people at mission control, each of them monitoring a specific aspect of the flight, to find out if each system was a "go" or a "no go." When every one of the controllers reported that his department was a "go," Charlesworth had the final determination. "I think one of the biggest decisions I have to make," he said, "is to commit three men to go to the moon from the earth orbit. The business of lunar flight is a whole new ball game. In earth orbit you are at most thirty minutes away from home in case of trouble, but now you are talking about days away from home and there may be some hard tradeoffs."

Charlesworth turned to Collins and told him to let Borman, Lovell, and Anders know that they were cleared to attempt to break out of Earth orbit and head for the moon. Fully aware of the historic significance, Collins contacted the spacecraft and stated simply, "Apollo 8, you are go for TLI." Later, Collins would state, "I can remember at the time thinking, 'Jeez, there's got to be a better way of saying this,' but we had our technical jargon and so I said, 'Apollo 8, you're go for TLI.' . . . I mean, there has to be a better way, don't you think, of saying that?' Yet that was our technical jargon."

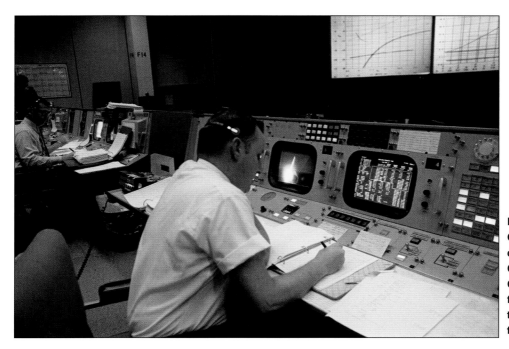

Flight director Cliff Charlesworth works at his console in the Mission Control Center. It was Charlesworth who gave the final go-ahead for Apollo 8 to leave Earth orbit and head for the moon.

PAVING THE WAY FOR APOLLO 8

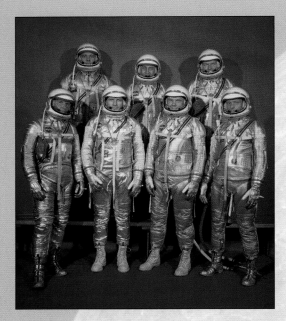

The Apollo 8 mission was the eighteenth crewed spaceflight launched by the United States, part of the third distinct program in NASA's space effort. The first program, named Project Mercury in reference to the wing-footed Roman god of travel, was carried out from 1958 to 1963. Its purpose was simple: to put an astronaut into space and return him back to Earth safely. Beginning with Alan Shepard's fifteen-minute flight on *Freedom 7* on May 5, 1961, NASA flew six crewed Mercury missions. The first two were suborbital, reaching space but returning to Earth without completing a full orbit of the planet. The most notable Mercury flight was on February 20, 1962, when John Glenn became the first American to orbit the Earth.

Top: The first seven American astronauts. Front row, left to right: Walter Schirra, Deke Slayton, John Glenn, Scott Carpenter. Back row, left to right: Alan Shepard, Gus Grissom, Gordon Cooper

Bottom: John Glenn enters the space capsule *Friendship 7* prior to his historic 1962 flight.

The second of NASA's human spaceflight programs was Gemini, which took its name—Latin for "twins"—from the constellation because the Gemini space capsule carried two astronauts. The Gemini Project, which took place in 1965 and 1966, was designed to pave the way for landing an American on the moon. Its missions studied what happened when astronauts spent many days in space and how well astronauts could operate outside their spacecraft and practiced linking two separate spacecraft in space.

Project Apollo was named for the Greek and Roman god of music, poetry, art, oracles, archery, medicine, sun, light, and knowledge. This third program was to use the knowledge and experience gained by the Mercury and Gemini Projects to place an American on the moon. Apollo 1 was intended to be the first crewed Apollo flight, but after the tragic, fatal fire during testing, no crewed flights were launched until Apollo 7, which was notable as well for featuring the first live telecast from a crewed spacecraft.

The second crewed Apollo flight was Apollo 8.

Astronaut Alan Shepard receives the NASA Distinguished Service Medal from President John F. Kennedy after becoming the first American to fly in space.

Lovell, Anders, and Borman received Collins's transmission two hours and twenty-seven minutes into their flight. Now, ten seconds before attempting to refire the SPS engine, their computer—which had less power than one of today's inexpensive handheld calculators—asked them one last time if they wanted to go ahead with the maneuver. Lovell tapped in the command for the engine to fire. At 9:41 a.m. (Houston time) on December 21, as Apollo 8 passed over Hawaii, the SPS engine began a burn that lasted five minutes and eighteen seconds. When it ended, Apollo 8's speed had increased from 17,000 to 24,200 miles per hour, breaking it out of Earth's orbit. Frank Borman, Jim Lovell, and Bill Anders were now truly on their way to the moon, and they were moving faster than any human beings had ever traveled before.

As soon as the SPS burn had been successfully completed, Lovell radioed the information to mission control. "You're on your way," Chris Kraft immediately radioed back. "You're *really* on your way!" Gene Kranz had a more emotional reaction: "When I heard the crew report the maneuver's completion," he said, "it really hit me. I had to get up and walk outside because I was so happy I was crying."

As for the astronauts, "we sweated the burn into lunar orbit," Lovell wrote later. "If that burn time was not correct we could have gone into all sorts of oddball orbits, none of them nice. When we committed ourselves to it we were really saying, 'Earth, we are forsaking you. We're going into the influence of the moon, and if that engine doesn't work when we want to leave here, we are going to belong to the moon forever.'"

Lovell and the others had the gigantic challenges of putting Apollo 8 into orbit around the moon still to come. By the time Apollo 8 got in the vicinity of the moon, it would have traveled almost a quarter of a million miles. If the path the spacecraft had taken had been off by even the slightest fraction, the spacecraft would crash against the lunar surface. Several of the world's leading mathematicians had studied the problem, but none could guarantee that the calculations were as accurate as they needed to be. And even if the trajectory had been correct, the critical procedure of firing the SPS engine for exactly the right amount of time to slow the spacecraft down and set it into lunar orbit would have to take place on the far side of the moon, out of radio contact with the Earth. "The moon," said Andrew Chaikin, "is moving along in its orbit at thousands of miles an hour. . . . You're trying to zip ahead of the leading edge of the moon, whip around the back side, fire your engine, and go into orbit just sixty-nine miles above the surface. You know, sixty-nine miles out of 230,000 . . . doesn't leave you a lot of room for error."

No one was more aware of the dangers than Commander Borman. And he had a specific concern. "It was," he later wrote, "a delicate maneuver putting a spacecraft into orbit around the Moon, but one that was critical to the success of a human landing there. The problem is that if you don't put on the brakes at the right moment for the right length of time, you'll fly away from Earth for eternity."

Borman was prepared to deal with the dangers and risks. He was not prepared for getting sick. Getting himself, his crew, and the spacecraft ready for the first crewed orbit of the moon had tired him out more than he had realized at first, and, as he later told an interviewer, "I did something . . . that I had stated pretty firmly I would never do: I took a sleeping pill. We had a little difficulty keeping out of the way of the spent third stage of our rocket on the way out, and that made me two hours late getting down for my sleep period. I knew we all had to be rested when we got to the moon, so I took a pill. It worked, but I woke up about five hours later with a headache and nausea. I actually threw up a couple of times, and I thought I should tell the ground. Now, one of the difficulties of communicating with the ground is that everything we say is broadcast so that anyone can hear, and sometimes little hints of illnesses are overplayed. So I informed the ground about my problem only reluctantly."

MOONSTRUCK

Humans have always been insatiably curious about the moon. Few things have inspired as much mythology and imagination as our nearest neighbor in space. Mysterious for tens of thousands of years, the moon was credited with attributes as varied as being the resting place of the gods, causing madness, and even bringing werewolves to life.

Many ancient societies built great observatories to chart the path of the moon as well as that of the sun, planets, and stars. Around 400 BCE, astronomers in Babylon invented the earliest zodiac, a system to divide the year into lunar periods and, not so incidentally, to assign prophetic significance to the period of a person's birth. In the Americas, ancient Navajo credited the First Man and the First Woman with making the moon and the sun to provide light for the world. The ancient Greeks believed that the moon was a planet, very much like Earth. "The moon appears to be terrestrial," wrote Greek historian and essayist Plutarch, "for she is inhabited like the earth . . . and peopled with the greatest living creatures and fairest plants." Among the most enduring of all the lunar legends, one embraced by many cultures, involved cheese. Because the moon often looks like a round of green or unripened cheese with pockmarks and divots, many people across the world were convinced that it might well be made of green cheese.

In the late 1500s and early 1600s, the Italian astronomer-scientist Galileo Galilei, following in the footsteps of the earlier Polish astronomer-mathematician Nicolaus Copernicus and taking advantage of the newly invented telescope, produced a more accurate description of a solar system than any created before. Galileo's findings gave rise to speculation about travel to the moon and potential encounters with people and creatures living there and inspired the first wave—of an eventual flood—of books about imaginary lunar voyages. Among the first was Johannes Kepler's 1634 novel *Somnium* (*The Dream*), in which visitors to the moon come face-to-face with serpentine creatures. Kepler's book was a great success and was followed by a spate of other moon voyage novels, among them Cyrano de Bergerac's *Histoire comique des états et empires de la lune* (*A Comical History of the States and Empires of the Moon*), published in 1657, in which several attempts are made to reach the lunar surface, culminating with the main character being launched to the moon by explosives—the first fictitious character to reach the moon by means of a rocket.

Over the next two centuries, science fiction became an increasingly popular way to explore the possibilities of the moon. Among the most widely read works was Edward Everett Hale's nineteenth-century short story "The Brick Moon."

Of all these books and short stories, the most famous is Jules Verne's *From the Earth to the Moon*. Aside from the intriguing plot, the book is noteworthy for predicting, almost exactly one hundred years before Apollo 8, that people from the United States would be the first to set foot on the moon, that their spacecraft would be launched from Florida, that it would splash down in the Pacific, and that its astronauts would be recovered by the United States Navy.

Actually, it was not Borman but Lovell and Anders, using a private radio channel to avoid alerting the public, who let NASA officials know that their commander was not feeling well. The officials did not take the news lightly. If there was a virus aboard Apollo 8, it threatened all three astronauts and there would be no choice but to abort the mission and bring them home as quickly as possible. Fortunately, while NASA doctors were huddling with Christopher Kraft and George Low, Borman began to feel better, and, with their vital input, the decision was made to continue the flight.

Borman's return to health came just in time for him to participate in the first of Apollo 8's six televised broadcasts from space. From the beginning, Borman had opposed bringing a television camera aboard the spacecraft. In his opinion, it added unnecessary weight to the craft, and he was convinced that telecasts from space would interfere with the crew's far more important duties. But NASA had overruled him. It would turn out to be one of the best overrules the agency would ever make.

The first Apollo 8 telecast took place at two p.m. (Houston time) on Sunday, December 22. The black-and-white camera was one of the world's first handheld video cameras and weighed about four and a half pounds on Earth. The presentation opened with a shot of a smiling Bill Anders staring at a toothbrush that was floating freely in front of him in the weightless atmosphere. Then Frank Borman's voice broke in, stating, "This transmission is coming to you approximately halfway between the moon and the Earth. We have been thirty-one hours and about twenty minutes into the flight. We have about less than forty hours left to go to the moon. You can see Bill's got his toothbrush here. He's has been brushing his teeth regularly to demonstrate how things float around in zero g"—referring to gravitational pull, measured as a multiple of Earth's gravity. The camera also revealed Jim Lovell in the command module's lower bay, preparing chocolate pudding for the next meal's dessert.

Bill Anders practices moving about in weight-lessness during the Apollo 8 flight. For Anders, the only rookie aboard, everything on the flight was new.

The first Apollo 8 telecast was supposed to provide viewers with an unprecedented view of the Earth from space, but when Anders attached the telephoto lens to the camera, he discovered that the lens was defective. "I certainly wish we could show you the Earth," Borman stated. "It is a beautiful view, with predominantly blue background and just huge covers of white clouds."

The telecast ended with a close-up of Jim Lovell, as Borman explained, to "let everyone see he has already outdistanced us in the beard race." Apollo 8's first telecast lasted only fifteen minutes and had failed to show the public a view of the Earth from space. But even without the views of the Earth, the telecast had a dramatic effect on its millions of viewers. Throughout the nation and in many other parts of the world, the reality began to sink in that these men were alone more than 135,000 miles out in space and were moving farther away with every passing minute. The telecast had outraged many TV viewers by preempting a National Football League game, but millions of others had been made aware that something very special, something historic, was taking place.

The telecast had a particularly strong effect on Frank Borman, who realized that he had been wrong to oppose taking a television camera aboard. "I said 'no' a lot," he later stated, "and the nice thing about it was that NASA gave the commander enough prerogative that they backed him up. I was overruled on one thing and that was because management was a lot smarter than I was. I didn't want to take the damn television camera with me. And they said, 'Let's take it,' and they were right. . . . It turned out to be so important because we could share what we saw with the world. . . . We were cutting out everything, even down to the extra meals, which weighed sixteen ounces or something like that. But I was very shortsighted there, and NASA was right."

Only a day after the initial telecast, Apollo 8 conducted a repeat performance. And this time the telephoto lens worked, enabling viewers to become the first in history ever to see live televised pictures of the Earth as a globe.

The highlight of the second telecast came when Lovell said, "What I keep imagining is, if I'm some lonely traveler from another planet, what I think about the Earth at this altitude, whether I think it'd be inhabited or not. . . . I was just kind of curious whether I would land on the blue or brown part of the Earth."

To which Anders quipped, "You better hope that we land on the blue part."

This view of Earth was sent from space during Apollo 8's second live television transmission. At the time, the spacecraft was some 176,533 miles from Earth.

A WHOLE
NEW WORLD

TUESDAY, DECEMBER 24, 1968. At 3:53 a.m. (Houston time), two days and twenty hours into its unprecedented flight, Apollo 8 curved around the moon. As Frank Borman, Bill Anders, and Jim Lovell became the first humans to see the dark side of the moon, the spacecraft lost all contact with Earth.

It was time to put Apollo 8 into lunar orbit. Back at mission control, everyone knew that if the SPS burn was successful, Apollo 8 would emerge from behind the moon in thirty-six minutes. No one dared express what would happen if the SPS failed to function properly. "We had loss of signal as they went around behind the moon," retro fire officer Jerry Bostick would later recall. "And it was rather depressing all of a sudden. It was a letdown, like, Well, what's going on? Well, we don't know. We can't talk to them. And the first thing I heard was from [Flight Director] Glynn Lunney, who said, 'This is probably a good time for everyone to take a break.' And I thought, 'That's the dumbest thing I've ever heard. How can we take a break when the spacecraft and the guys

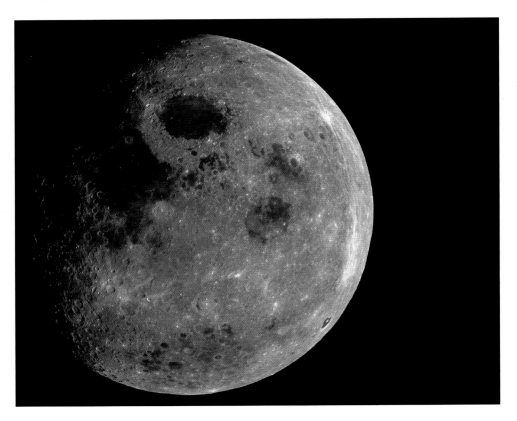

Before Apollo 8, humans had never been able to take such close-up photographs of the moon. This picture was taken by Bill Anders shortly before the spacecraft entered lunar orbit.

are on the dark side of the moon?' And he said, 'Well, there's nothing much we can do to help 'em now, and we have a few minutes here, so it's a good time to take a break.' "

At 4:59 a.m. (Houston time) on December 24, 1968, ten minutes after losing communication with the Earth, Lovell fired the SPS engine. The engine ignited without incident and burned flawlessly. When the maneuver was over, Apollo 8 was in an elliptical lunar orbit. It was an amazing achievement, but, for Bill Anders, one that called for reflection as well. "It occurred to me," he would later write, "that not only were we the first space travelers to enter another body's gravitational sphere of influence, but also we were the first to cut off our ties with the earth by allowing ourselves to be 'captured' [by the gravitational pull of a different body]."

"Suddenly," Anders recalled, "we saw millions of stars, more than you could see in a planetarium, to the point where it confused the constellations. So that was rather spectacular. And I remember looking at them because I was interested in astronomy, and then I looked kind of over my left shoulder and suddenly, the stars stopped. And there was this big black void, black hole. And that was the moon! . . . That was the only time in the flight the hair kind of came up on the back of my neck a little bit."

Describing the moments immediately after the successful SPS burn, Jim Lovell stated, "On the computer then it said words to the effect 'You are now in lunar orbit. Your orbit is 60 by 130 nautical miles.' We all looked out the window but we didn't see any moon. All we saw was black velvet sky. And then we rotated the spacecraft around 180 degrees and there, slowly slipping by, were the ancient old craters on the far side of the moon, just about sixty miles below."

Being so close to the moon, Lovell remembered, "we were like three school kids looking into a candy store window. I think we forgot the flight plan. We

Above: Command module pilot Jim Lovell at his guidance and navigation station

Right: Among the most spectacular of the lunar landscapes captured by cameras aboard Apollo 8 were those showing the moon's many craters. The large crater in the foreground of this picture is named Goclenius.

had our noses pressed against the glass. We were looking at those craters go by, you know. It was a really amazing sight."

As Bill Anders later wrote, "I had developed a mind's-eye view of what I was going to see, but I was surprised. On the moon's near side, the one we have seen and studied from earth for centuries, sights were familiar. But on the back side, where no man has ever looked before, it was different from what I had expected. It looked like a battlefield, hole upon hole upon crater upon crater. I had expected some mountains, or cliffs, or sharp features. There were few, if any. The surface was pulverized, completely bashed. There was a total lack of sharp definition. The areas had just been beaten and beaten, over the eons, by meteorites. The closer I looked, the more craters I saw—an ever-increasing number of holes with ever-decreasing diameter."

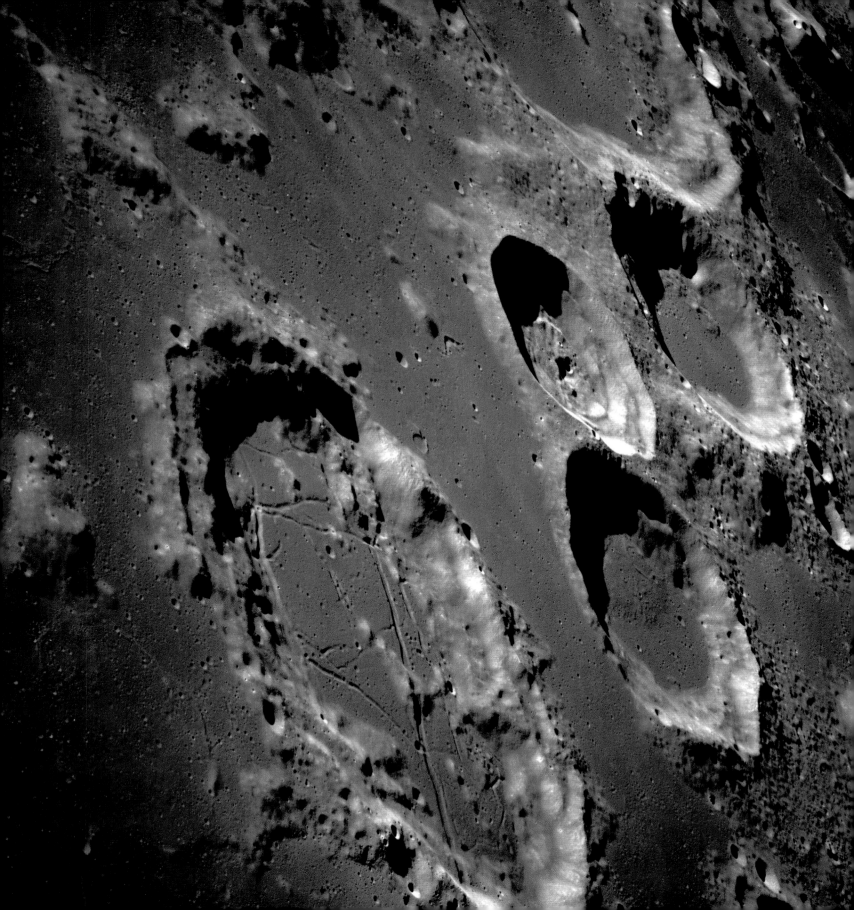

"What I saw flashing beneath us," Anders continued, "gave me a sense of real adventure, of exploration. I am sure it must have been the same thrill felt by Lewis and Clark, Byrd, Hillary, and many others as their own goals came into view. To me, and I think to many Americans, there has always been a sense of exploration and a sense of the frontier. The Appalachian Trail, the wide Missouri, Antarctica . . . they were there, and men came to conquer them and benefit from them. Now space is our frontier, and there I was in the lead wagon."

Sixty miles above the moon, Borman, Lovell, and Anders knew that the SPS had fired successfully, but back on Earth, millions of people did not. Then, precisely when it should have, the spacecraft reemerged and reestablished contact with mission control. Joyously, Paul Haney, manning the public information console, announced, "We got it! We've got it! Apollo 8 now in lunar orbit."

In mission control, Jerry Bostick went from frustration to jubilation. "When we heard from the crew within a second of the time that we expected to," he recalled, "it was one of the happiest moments of my life. We had been working for six or seven years to accomplish this. And there we were! We were in lunar orbit!"

The astronauts were surprised by the back side of the moon, but home on Earth, tens of millions of people were in a greater state of amazement at the still-almost-incomprehensible fact that humans had reached the moon. Included among them were the American astronauts' bitterest rivals. Nikolai Kamanin, the head of the Soviet cosmonaut corps, and some of his fellow cosmonauts were traveling on Christmas Eve when they rounded a corner and saw the bright crescent moon. Kamanin remembered later that they were well aware that three Americans were circling that very moon. "Everyone grew silent for a minute," he later said. The cosmonauts on that bus were filled with contradictory feelings: admiration for Borman, Lovell, and Anders and their accomplishment, but also disappointment that it was not Russians who were first to the moon.

Across the globe but also among those most deeply affected were the three Apollo 8 astronauts' wives. "It was Christmas Eve," recalled Marilyn Lovell. "I got in the car and was driving home and there was the moon. It was just absolutely beautiful. I looked at it and I thought, 'Oh my Lord, they're there. . . . My husband is going around that moon at this moment.'"

Her husband shared her sense of wonder. With Apollo 8 beginning its first lunar orbit, Jim Lovell remarked, "Well, did you guys ever think that one Christmas Eve you'd be orbiting the moon?" Ever aware of the challenges that still lay ahead, particularly the dangers of blasting their way out of lunar orbit, Bill Anders had a simple response. "Just hope," he replied, "we're not doing it on New Year's."

A TEAM EFFORT

"Thousands of people," Frank Borman later declared, "made this possible." If anything, thousands was an understatement. The Apollo project was made possible by some four hundred thousand people. As Bill Anders stated, "The Apollo 8 crew gets 99 percent of the laurels and the pat-on-the-backs and the interviews . . . and headlines, but we have said with real feeling that we were just the tip of the iceberg. There were hundreds of people in mission control and in launch control. . . . There were thousands of people in the contractor network."

The hundreds of thousands of men and women who designed, developed, and made the millions of parts that went into the Saturn V rocket and the Apollo 8 spacecraft were located in all fifty states. The Saturn V was built at the Marshall Space Flight Center in Huntsville, Alabama. Apollo 8's command and service modules were constructed at North American Rockwell in Downey, California. The computers on board and in mission control were built by workers at IBM in New York and programmed at Draper Labs at MIT in Cambridge, Massachusetts. The all-important navigation systems relied on simulations by scientists and astronomers at the Morehead Planetarium at the University of North Carolina.

As commander of Apollo 8, Borman was grateful not only for the skill of those who contributed to the mission but also for their dedication. "I can remember going through a factory at midnight," he later recalled. "We spent a lot of time going through factories and talking to people about zero defects, and one wonderful woman . . . grabbed me and hugged me and gave me a kiss and said, 'You don't worry, we're all on the same team and we're all going to do our job.'"

Most important of all were the hundreds of people in mission control charged with making sure the three astronauts arrived at their destination, completed their mission, and returned safely. The Apollo 8 astronauts had tremendous faith in the abilities of flight director Chris Kraft. "Chris Kraft," stated Anders, "is . . . very disciplined, very competent, and an extremely good manager. We couldn't have had a better guy running the flight control because he ran it with discipline, with expertise, but he also ran it with compassion." Author Andrew Chaikin described Kraft as "like a cherished battlefield commander . . . the guy you'd want to lead you into battle. And the thing about Kraft that was so amazing to people was that he gave them responsibility, awesome responsibility. . . . Most of these flight controllers were in their twenties or their thirties and here was Kraft saying. 'Well, young man, what do you think we should do?'"

Kraft's team of flight controllers sat in tiered rows in the aptly named control room. The controllers with the most vital tasks sat at the consoles in the first row. "We call the first row in the control center 'the trench,'" explained Jerry Bostick. "There's a debate about how it really got its name but it's the lowest row of consoles in the control center and we called it 'the first line of defense in manned space flight.' We were the guys in the trench: the retro fire officer, the flight dynamics officer and the guidance officer. We were the ground pilots, if you will, who tracked the spacecraft, calculated the maneuvers and told the astronauts what time to burn, what maneuvers to do and where to go. So, we were a proud bunch."

Central to the team effort that characterized the Apollo 8 mission were the scientists, engineers, and astronauts who manned the consoles in the Mission Control Center.

EARTHRISE

IT WAS CHRISTMAS EVE, and Apollo 8 was coming out from behind the moon for the fourth time. As planned, Borman rolled the spacecraft so that Lovell could do a navigational sighting. As he completed the roll, with his window facing the lunar horizon, Borman noticed a blue-and-white arch edging up from behind the moon's horizon. The arch soon turned into a growing sphere. "Oh, my God!" Borman cried. "Look at that picture over there! Here's the earth coming up! Wow, is that pretty."

Taken just before Bill Anders's more famous picture, Borman's image was overlooked for nearly thirty years because it was black-and-white.

All three astronauts had been taken completely by surprise. "We were trained to go to the moon," Anders later explained. "We were focused on the moon, observing the moon, studying the moon, and the Earth was not really in our thoughts until it popped up above that horizon." Despite all the preparations that had gone into the Apollo 8 mission, no one had given a thought to photographing the Earth from lunar orbit. But as they stared out the windows, it suddenly occurred to all three men. Borman was the first to grab a camera loaded with black-and-white film and take a photograph. Anders, aware that his commander always insisted that everything be done exactly as planned, took the opportunity to poke good-natured fun at Borman and joked, "Hey, don't take that — it's not scheduled."

Joking aside, Anders then asked Borman to hand him the camera so that he could take his own pictures. But as he gazed at the sight of the rising Earth, the only colorful object in the vast blackness of space, he realized that whatever pictures he took had to be taken in color.

Quickly Anders yelled over to Lovell, asking him to get a roll of color film. Things grew tense as Lovell rooted through the storage locker trying to find the film while Anders shouted, "C'mon, hurry up — we don't have much time." Finally, Lovell found the film. As Anders framed his shot, Lovell crowded in next to him at the window, urging him to start shooting. "Wait a minute," Anders replied. "Just let me get the right setting here now. Just calm down. Calm down, Lovell." Anders then snapped the shutter and took a photograph that would, as author Drew Dellinger has expressed it, "forever change our image of the planet and ourselves." It would become one of the most famous and most reproduced photographs of all time.

As the Earth drifted slowly out of view, the three astronauts grew reflective. They had just witnessed the first earthrise ever seen by a human being. "The view of the earth from the moon fascinated me," Borman would later explain, "a small disk, 240,000 miles away. It was hard to think that that little thing

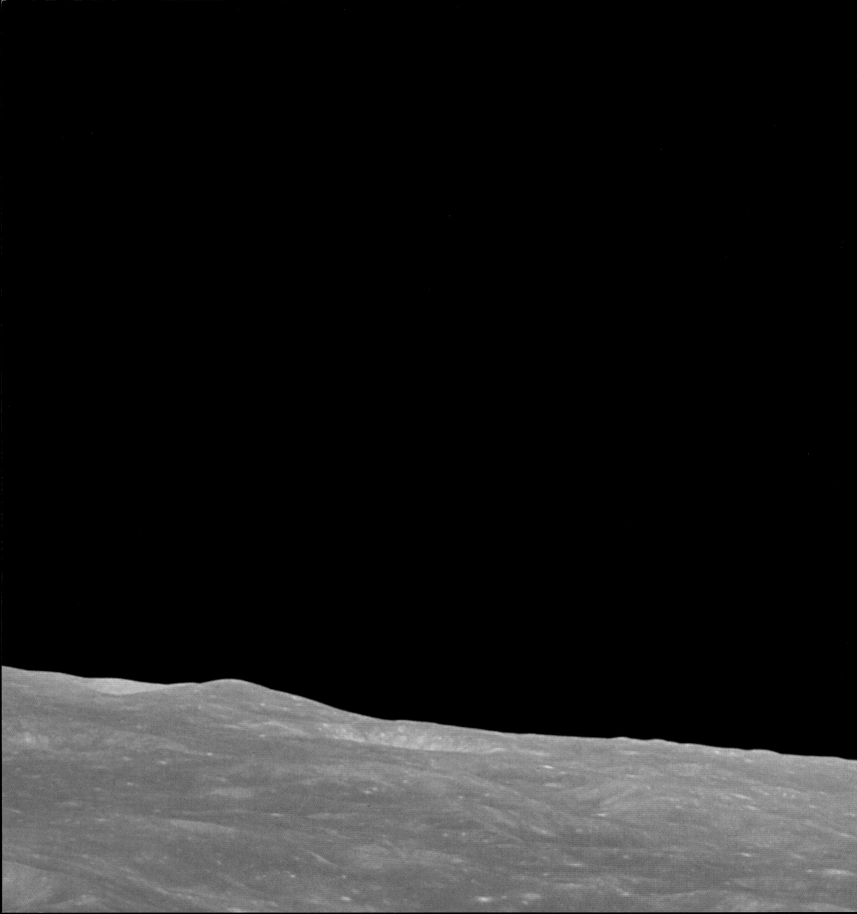

held so many problems, so many frustrations. Raging nationalistic interests, famines, wars, pestilence don't show from that distance. I'm convinced that some wayward stranger in a spacecraft, coming from some other part of the heavens, could look at earth and never know that it was inhabited at all. But the same wayward stranger would certainly know instinctively that if the earth *were* inhabited, then the destinies of all who lived on it must inevitably be interwoven and joined. We are one hunk of ground, water, air, clouds, floating around in space. From out there it really is 'one world.'"

Anders would always remember that "when I looked up and saw the Earth coming up on this very stark, beat-up lunar horizon, an Earth that was the only color that we could see, a very fragile-looking Earth, a very delicate-looking Earth, I was immediately almost overcome by the thought that here we came all this way to the Moon, and yet the most significant thing we're seeing is our home planet, the Earth."

Lovell had a different reaction to the Earthrise. "We came around the moon . . . and all of a sudden we saw the earth come out of a lunar horizon; and that was really a significant sight for me because I could put my thumb up to the window of the spacecraft and completely hide the earth. I realized that everything I had ever known, my home, my loved ones, everything that was there that I had known about is behind my thumb. I realized at that time just how insignificant we are in the universe."

In 1948, a full twenty years before Apollo 8, British astronomer Sir Fred Hoyle predicted that "Once a photograph of the Earth, taken from the outside, is available . . . a new idea as powerful as any in history will be let loose." Hoyle's remarkable prediction began to come true soon after Apollo 8 returned to Earth, as Anders's photograph, which had been titled *Earthrise,* came to symbolize the lessons learned from human beings' first voyage to another world. The Apollo 8 astronauts had indeed taken a picture that would forever change our image of our planet and ourselves.

"Look again at that dot," noted astrophysicist and author Carl Sagan would write. "That's here, that's home, that's us. On it everyone you love, everyone you know, everyone you ever heard of, every human being who ever was, lived out their lives. The aggregate of our joy and suffering, thousands of confident religions, ideologies and economic doctrines, every hunter and forager, every hero and coward, every creator and destroyer of civilization, every king and peasant, every young couple in love, every mother and father, hopeful child, inventor and explorer, every teacher of morals, every corrupt politician, every 'superstar,' every 'supreme leader,' every saint and sinner in the history of our species lived there—on a mote of dust suspended in a sunbeam."

To many, like Lovell, the Earthrise photograph became a symbol of the Earth's fragility, a reminder of just how small and insignificant the Earth's place in the universe truly is. Walter Cronkite found this a great lesson to be learned. "I think that picture of the earthrise of the moon's horizon, that blue disk out there in space, floating alone in the darkness, the utter black of space, had the effect of impressing on all of us our loneliness out here," he reflected. "The fact that we seem to be the only spot where anything like humans could be living. And . . . the major impression I think it made on most of us was the fact, how ridiculous it is that we have this difficulty getting along on this little lifeboat of ours floating out there in space, and the necessity of our understanding each other and of the brotherhood of humankind on this floating island of ours, made a great impression, I think, on everybody."

Out of the scores of commentary that *Earthrise* elicited, one remains the best remembered and most often quoted. Written by poet Archibald MacLeish, printed first in the *New York Times* and then in publications throughout Europe, it was titled "Riders on the Earth."

"For the first time in all of time," MacLeish wrote, "men have seen the Earth: seen it not as continents or oceans from the little distance of a hundred miles or two or three, but seen it from the depths of space; seen it whole and round and beautiful and small. . . . To see the Earth as it truly is, small and blue and beautiful in that eternal silence where it floats, is to see ourselves as riders on the Earth together, brothers on that bright loveliness in the eternal cold—brothers who know that they are truly brothers."

There is no question that *Earthrise* raised worldwide consciousness about the fragility of Earth itself in a way unlike anything that had come before. As Carl Sagan put it, "Our planet is a lonely speck in the great enveloping cosmic dark. There is no hint that help will come from elsewhere to save us from ourselves."

A new determination sprang from this new awareness of the Earth's fragility. "We should cherish our home planet," urged the *Christian Science Monitor*. "Men must conserve the Earth's resources. They must protect their planetary environment from spreading pollution. They have no other sanctuary in the solar system. This, perhaps, is the most pertinent message for all of us that the astronauts bring back from the Moon." Will Pomerantz, vice president of special projects at Virgin Galactic, put it this way: "How can you look at a picture like that . . . and not realize we live on a small world! That we need to be good stewards of our environment, that we need to be good neighbours to the other seven billion people trapped here on this pale blue dot."

Just as Fred Hoyle had predicted, a powerful new idea had indeed been unleashed. Thanks to *Earthrise,* a great new era of ecology and environmental consciousness was born. "Looking back," author Robert Poole has observed, "it is possible to see that 'Earthrise' marked the tipping point, the moment when the sense of the space age flipped from what it meant for space to what it meant for the Earth."

The impact of *Earthrise* was felt by people everywhere. "I date my own reawakening of interest in man's environment to the Apollo 8 mission and to the first clear photographs of Earth from that mission," wrote John Caffrey, a correspondent for *Science* magazine. "I suspect that the greatest lasting benefit of the Apollo missions may be, if my hunch is correct, this sudden rush of inspiration to try to save this fragile environment—the whole one—if we still can."

Even before the Earthrise photograph, some individuals and organizations worked to foster environmental awareness. One such organization, the Nature Conservancy, was established in 1951 to protect ecologically important lands and waters around the world. In 1956, the Sierra Club gained national attention for successfully halting the construction of an environmentally damaging dam on the Colorado River. And in 1962, Rachel Carson's book *Silent Spring* aroused the public interest against the overuse of pesticides.

And then came *Earthrise,* and the environmental movement was truly set into motion. The United States celebrated its first Earth Day in 1970, and it soon erupted into a national event with twenty million participants. In the same year, the National Environmental Policy Act became law, major amendments were added to strengthen the Clean Air Act, and the Environmental Protection Agency was established. In 1972, the first United Nations Conference on the Environment was held in Stockholm, Sweden. One year later, the United States Congress passed the Endangered Species Act.

Jim Lovell marveled at *Earthrise*'s impact. "I thought it would be a great picture, but I didn't comprehend that, in today's language, it would go viral—that it would be the capstone and message of the mission."

PHOTOGRAPHS THAT CHANGED THE WORLD

Almost from its first public viewing, *Earthrise* became one of the most influential photographs ever taken. It was only the latest in a line of pictures that, from the birth of photography in 1839, made an enormous impact on people's thoughts and actions.

The Civil War was the first American armed conflict to be photographed. When the war began, the North and the South each believed that theirs would be a quick and easy victory. Both sides marched off to war as if they were embarking upon a great adventure. Meanwhile, Mathew Brady, America's most famous photographer at the time, organized a team of some twenty photographers and sent them to the battlefields to record the conflict. Although the cameras of the day could not capture action, Brady's team took thousands of photographs of armies drilling, of enormous weapons, and of soldiers, including thousands of young boys, caught up in the most tragic and desperate of struggles. The images from Brady's photographic corps quickly revealed something very different from the great adventure both sides had expected. And one image in particular would have an enormous impact.

The photographer was Timothy O'Sullivan, who would later become one of the world's greatest landscape photographers. The publisher of the picture was Alexander Gardner, who would himself take more than 1,200 photographs before the war was over, including a number of the most famous images of Abraham Lincoln. In his book *Sketchbook of the Civil War,* Gardner titled O'Sullivan's picture *A Harvest of Death* and accompanied it with a caption that read:

"Slowly, over the misty fields of Gettysburg . . . came the sunless morn, after the retreat by Lee's broken army. Through the shadowy vapors, it was, indeed, a 'harvest of death' that was presented. . . . Such a picture conveys a useful moral: It shows the blank horror and reality of war, in opposition to its pageantry. Here are the dreadful details! Let them aid in preventing such another calamity falling upon the nation."

O'Sullivan's photograph was sent directly from the battlefield to be displayed in Mathew Brady's highly popular photographic studio. Americans had never seen a photograph of dead soldiers before, and *A Harvest of Death* shocked them. Just as many of those who viewed *Earthrise* would never look at the Earth in the same way again, enormous numbers of those who came into contact with *A Harvest of Death* would never again regard war in the same manner.

A Harvest of Death, by photographer Timothy O'Sullivan. Soon after Alexander Gardner's *Sketchbook of the Civil War* was published in 1866, it became the Civil War's best-known visual record.

Almost seventy years after the Civil War ended, the United States faced another crisis, the Great Depression. Tens of millions of Americans found themselves unemployed and struggling to survive. A single photograph not only came to symbolize the Great Depression but also played a major role in inspiring changes aimed at preventing a disaster of that type from happening again.

It was taken by Dorothea Lange, destined to later become one of the world's most famous photographers, but at the time an employee of a federal agency now known as the Farm Security Administration. Through her pictures, Lange was determined to reveal the human side of those driven into hard times by the natural disasters that had turned a large swath of the United States into a giant dust bowl.

"Their roots were all torn out," Lange wrote. "The only background they had was a background of utter poverty. . . . I had to get my camera to register those things about those people that were more important than how poor they were—their pride, their strength, their spirit."

Lange traveled the nation's hardest-hit areas taking photographs that earned her the title "humanitarian with a camera." One day, she happened upon a migrant workers' camp and captured an image of a mother with three of her seven children. "I did not ask her name or her history," Lange later recounted. "She told me her age, that she was thirty-two. She said they had been living on frozen vegetables from the surrounding fields and birds that the children killed . . . There she sat in that lean-to tent with her children huddled around her, and seemed to know that my pictures might help her, and so she helped me."

Lange titled the picture *Migrant Mother.* Printed in scores of magazines and newspapers, it called attention to the plight of millions of people and gave Congress new motivation to pass laws that helped relieve the situation.

Migrant Mother was one in a series of photographs that Dorothea Lange took of Florence Owens Thompson and her children in February or March 1936 in Nipomo, California.

AN EXTRAORDINARY BROADCAST

THE CREW OF APOLLO 8 had been in lunar orbit for nearly fourteen hours and had orbited the moon nine times. In six hours, after one more orbit, they would attempt to blast out of moon orbit and head back to Earth. It was nearing time for a scheduled Christmas Eve telecast that promised to be the most watched event of the entire mission.

A view of the far side of the moon from Apollo 8. The dark-floored crater near the middle of the right side of the photograph is about forty-five miles wide.

But Borman had a serious concern: Lovell and Anders were getting tired. He couldn't help noticing weariness in Lovell's voice. And Lovell had been making some mistakes. More than once he had punched the wrong command into the computer. Moving from window to window, taking pictures, Anders was also not acting as alert as he had up to this point in the flight.

As commander, Borman made a quick decision. When mission control radioed with some new tasks to be done, Borman responded that he was canceling all activities for the next couple of hours. "I'll stay up and keep the spacecraft vertical, and then take some . . . pictures," he radioed, "but I want Jim and Bill to get some rest."

Anders immediately protested that he was willing to try the new task from mission control. "No," responded Borman. "You try it, and then we'll make another mistake." When Lovell joined Anders in protest, Borman got even tougher. "I want you to get . . . in bed! Right now!" he ordered his pilot. Back at mission control, Mike Collins could clearly hear the exchange between Borman and his crew. Immediately, he radioed Borman to say that he and his colleagues on the ground agreed with the commander's decision. By this point in the flight, no one at mission control, at any level, was about to question Frank Borman's authority.

Two hours later, refreshed from their naps, Anders and Lovell rejoined Borman. It was time to get ready for their scheduled Christmas Eve message. NASA officials had asked that the telecast begin with the astronauts describing the moon while the camera was trained on the lunar surface.

For twenty minutes, Borman, Lovell, and Anders provided those on Earth with the first-ever live descriptions of the mountains and craters of the moon. Borman was first to speak. "This is Apollo 8 coming to you live from the moon. . . . We showed you first a view of the earth as we've been watching it for the past sixteen hours. Now we're switching so that we can show you the moon that we've been flying over . . . for the last sixteen hours. The moon is a different

At the time of the Apollo 8 flight, Jim Lovell
had spent more time in space than any other
human being. Still, the views of the moon from
only some sixty miles away would remain
among his most vivid space memories.

thing to each one of us," Borman continued after opening the telecast. "I think that each one carried his own impression of what he's seen today. I know my impression is that it's a vast, lonely, forbidding-type existence, or expanse of nothing. It looks rather like clouds and clouds of pumice stone and it certainly would not appear to be a very inviting place to live or work."

Lovell went next. "I think the best way to describe this area is a vastness of black and white—absolutely no color. . . . The vast loneliness up here at the moon is awe-inspiring, and it makes you realize what you have back there on earth. The earth from here is a grand oasis in the big vastness of space."

Last, it was Anders's turn. "I think the thing that impressed me the most was the lunar sunrises and sunsets. These in particular bring out the stark nature of the terrain," he said. "The sky up here is also a rather forbidding, foreboding expanse of blackness, with no stars visible when we're flying over the . . . moon in daylight. You can see that the moon has been bombarded through the eons with numerous meteorites. Every square inch is pockmarked." Finally, in a tone that reflected the awe he felt, Anders stated, "How finite the Earth looks. . . . There's no frame around it. It's hanging there, the only color in the black vastness of space, like a dust mote in infinity."

For the first time, millions and millions of people were able to witness a moment of exploration at the exact time it took place. "The thing about Apollo that sets it apart from every other event in the history of exploration," space historian Andrew Chaikin has written, "is that because it was happening live on television, humans could share in the event as it was happening. We didn't have to wait for the letters to come back from the western frontier, weeks and months later. We didn't have to wait until the explorers returned to hear about the adventure. We could see it with our own eyes and have our own experience. . . . That was an experience for all of us to share in. That was our piece of Apollo 8. That was the moment at which we felt like explorers. We felt the awe and the wonder that these three men were experiencing so far from their home planet."

WHAT'S IN A NAME

A truly remarkable variety of names, often unusual, have been given to the craters, mountains, and other physical features on the surface of the moon. The modern system of assigning names to lunar landmarks was devised in 1651 by Italian astronomer and priest Giovanni Battista Riccioli, whose map of the moon gave names to lunar features, most of which are still in use today. These include the large dark areas of the moon's surface, known as mares, which he named for weather or for states of mind, giving us the Sea of Rains and the Sea of Tranquility. He named many of the moon's huge craters for famous scientists, philosophers, mathematicians, and explorers, a tradition that continued when later astronomers named craters near the moon's poles for terrestrial polar explorers Roald Amundsen and Ernest Shackleton.

Before the space age, only the near side of the moon was visible and known. That changed in 1959 when the uncrewed Soviet spacecraft Luna 3 transmitted the first pictures of the far side of the moon. Not surprisingly, the Soviets named several newly discovered far side features for Russian heroes, such as rocketry pioneer Tsiolkovsky, and places, such as the Sea of Moscow.

The United States' Apollo program resulted in new names as well. Most notable were the Apollo Basin, a spectacular crater named to honor all the Apollo missions, and craters named for the individual crewmembers of Apollo 8 (Borman, Lovell, and Anders) and Apollo 11 (Armstrong, Aldrin, and Collins). Starting in 1919, a body of scientists known as the International Astronomical Union (IAU)

APOLLO 17
LANDING SITE

A photographic illustration showing a portion of the lunar near side. The black dot in the Taurus-Littrow area shows where Apollo 17 made its moon landing.

has been responsible for accepting or rejecting proposed names for lunar features. One of the most interesting proposals came from none other than Apollo 8's Jim Lovell, who proposed naming a small mountain next to the Sea of Tranquility Mount Marilyn in honor of his wife. The IAU has declined to give official recognition to the name, but NASA astronauts recognize it and gave it importance when the crew of Apollo 11 referred to the point where they began humans' first descent to the moon as Mount Marilyn.

The Apollo 8 astronauts' eyewitness description of the lunar surface set an important precedent. Television cameras had already begun delivering scenes of battles to the general population, much as Alexander Gardner's photographs had brought the Civil War into people's living rooms. From Apollo 8 on, no matter how remote an area was being explored or how dangerous an event was taking place, the public expected television to make them eyewitnesses to it.

When the astronauts finished their descriptions of the moon, they had only two minutes left before they would once again disappear behind the back side of the moon. It was time for them to deliver their Christmas message. Before they left Earth, NASA's assistant administrator for public affairs, Julian Scheer, had told Borman, "We figure more people will be listening to your voice than that of any other man in history." The question was what would Borman and Lovell and Anders say to such a mind-bogglingly huge audience, an audience that NASA predicted would be more than one billion people, or roughly one out of every four people on the planet.

To their credit, NASA officials made no attempt to tell Borman, Lovell, and Anders what to say. All the astronauts had been told was to say "something appropriate." But what was appropriate? Initially, Borman thought that a call for world peace would be suitable, but he became concerned about how that would be received coming from a military person while the nation was involved in a bitter war in Vietnam.

Lovell had been equally perplexed. His first thought was to rewrite the words to "'Twas the Night Before Christmas" or "Jingle Bells." But when he discussed it with Borman and Anders, that idea was quickly dismissed. "It was too flippant," Lovell later explained. "It did not match the event."

Anders, a devout Catholic, had suggested reading something about the meaning of Christmas. But Borman rejected that idea, reminding Anders that millions of the people watching the telecast would not be Christians. They needed something that spoke to everyone. After thinking it over, Anders agreed, saying that they wanted to make "a significant statement, that not just Christians and Jews would understand, but that all people, Buddhist, Hindu or atheist, would react to in a deep and moving way to help them remember this event of exploration."

But what would it be? A month before Apollo 8's launch, stressed over finding what to say to such an enormous audience, Borman sought help from a friend, Simon Bourgin. Bourgin, a former science policy adviser to the United States Information Agency, was one of the smartest individuals Borman had ever met.

But Bourgin also found himself having trouble picking an appropriate topic. Stymied in turn, he asked another friend, reporter Joe Laitin, for help. Like Bourgin and the three astronauts, Laitin struggled to come up with a solution. So much so that his wife found him at four o'clock in the morning on his living-room floor surrounded by books, including the Bible, desperately trying to find an answer.

Mrs. Laitin looked at the pile of books and then picked up a copy of the Bible. "Why don't they just read from the book of Genesis?" she asked. Taking the Bible from his wife, Laitin turned to the first page and realized that she had a perfect solution. Though they were not holy words to everyone on Earth, they spoke to billions of people and had a sense of majesty about them totally befitting the occasion.

Laitin immediately went to his study and typed out a letter to Bourgin suggesting the first ten lines of Genesis. Bourgin heartily agreed and sent the letter on to Borman, who knew at first glance that his problem had been solved. Lovell was similarly delighted, stating, "You couldn't ask for better. The words were the foundation of most of the world's religions."

"We are now approaching lunar sunset," Borman began, "and for all the people back on earth, the crew of Apollo 8 have a message that we would like to send to you."

Then Anders began what author Robert Zimmerman has called "the most

The bright-rayed crater in this Apollo 8 photograph is named Giordano Bruno, for a sixteenth-century Italian scientist. The dark-floored crater immediately below it is named Lomonosov, for an eighteenth-century Russian scientist, and is fifty miles wide.

profound Christmas prayer ever given by any member of the human race." "'In the beginning,'" read Anders, "'God created the heaven and the earth. And the earth was without form, and void; and darkness was upon the face of the deep. And the Spirit of God moved upon the face of the waters. And God said, Let there be light; and there was light. And God saw the light, that it was good: and God divided the light from the darkness.'"

At this point Anders gave way to Jim Lovell. "'And God called the light Day, and the darkness he called Night. And the evening and the morning were the first day. And God said, Let there be a firmament in the midst of the waters, and let it divide the waters from the waters. And God made the firmament, and divided the waters which were under the firmament from the waters which were above the firmament: and it was so. And God called the firmament Heaven. And the evening and the morning were the second day.'"

Finally, Frank Borman took up the reading: "'And God said, Let the waters under the heavens be gathered together unto one place, and let the dry land appear: and it was so. And God called the dry land Earth; and the gathering together of the waters called the Seas: and God saw that it was good.' And from the crew of Apollo 8, we close with good night, good luck, a Merry Christmas, and God bless all of you—all of you on the good Earth."

For many watching at home, it seemed as if Borman's words were hanging in the air as Apollo 8 slipped behind the moon and communication with the astronauts was lost. "For those moments," recalled Gene Kranz, "I felt the presence of creation and the Creator. Tears were on my cheeks."

Jerry Bostick, seated at his console in mission control, was similarly affected. "I've never seen this place so quiet," he recalled. "There was a big hush in here, and tears in a lot of eyes. It was just the perfect thing to do at the perfect time."

Even veteran journalists who thought themselves immune to emotional reactions on what they were reporting were overcome by the words from 250,000 miles away and sixty-nine miles above the moon. "You know," stated

Walter Cronkite, "I'm afraid that my first reaction was, 'Oh, this is a little too much, this is a little too dramatic.' I might even have thought, 'This is a little corny.' But by the time Borman had finished reading that excerpt from the Bible, I admit that I had tears in my eyes. It was really impressive and just the right thing to do at the moment. Just the right thing." Bill Anders had no doubt in his mind as to why it was "the right thing to do." "To me," he stated, "[the Genesis reading] was that we're trying to say something sort of fundamental. Something that will stop and grab people's guts and say, hey this isn't just a little whistle-around-the-Earth space shot; this is man's . . . first step away from his home planet. I mean, we're talking about a second Genesis, if you will."

For more than a billion people, it had been an extraordinary viewing and listening experience. Live pictures beamed back from the long-mysterious, long-alien moon. Verses recited by American heroes a quarter of a million miles away. They had more than met the task of delivering an "appropriate" Christmas message. Now they faced an even greater challenge. They had to get themselves safely home.

The United States Postal Service commemorated Apollo 8 with a stamp honoring the mission, the Earthrise photograph, and the astronauts' Christmas broadcast.

A DISSENTING VOICE

Apollo 8's Christmas message received acclaim from around the world. Not everyone, however, agreed with the choice of words the astronauts had read. One of the most outspoken was Madalyn Murray O'Hair, the founder and president of an atheism activist organization called American Atheists. In 1960, when the required recitation of prayers and in-class Bible readings were common in schools across America, O'Hair gained worldwide attention for suing the Baltimore schools, arguing that these practices violated the Constitution's clause against the establishment of religion. The case reached the United States Supreme Court. In 1963, the Court ruled eight to one in favor of O'Hair's petition, which had been joined by a similar case, effectively ending school-sanctioned Bible reading and compulsory prayer in the nation's public schools.

The decision made O'Hair extremely unpopular, so much so that in 1964, *Life* magazine reported that she was "the most hated woman in America." In December 1968, O'Hair brought a similar suit in light of the Apollo 8 astronauts' Bible reading. Eventually the Supreme Court dismissed O'Hair's suit due to lack of jurisdiction.

Madalyn Murray O'Hair made headlines when she attempted to prevent further Bible readings from space. Tragically, she made the news again in 1995, when she, her son, and her granddaughter were kidnapped and murdered by a convicted felon out on parole.

RETURN
TO EARTH

AS SOON AS Frank Borman delivered the last words of the Christmas Eve telecast, he and his crew were all business as they quickly began organizing themselves for the final firing of the SPS engine that would, if all went well, blast Apollo 8 out of lunar orbit and set it on a path for home.

This Apollo 8 photograph, taken as the crew headed home from the first orbit of the moon by humans, shows a half-illuminated Earth with the sun reflecting off the Indian Ocean.

Preparations took some two and a half hours. Once they emerged from the moon's shadow, all three astronauts listened intently as Ken Mattingly in mission control, an astronaut on the support crew, relayed the data they needed for the SPS burn. With the data entered into their computer and their clocks set at Houston time, they went around the spacecraft storing every loose piece of equipment.

The SPS engine had been fired to put Apollo 8 into lunar orbit a day earlier with the spacecraft on the far side of the moon. For the safest and most efficient return to Earth, reignition of the engine to blast the craft out of moon orbit would also need to take place on the dark side, with the astronauts out of contact with the Earth.

As always, the astronauts were well aware of the dangers. "I think," Frank Borman would later state, "the premier of all the tense moments was the burn to get us back out of lunar orbit. We only had a single engine to do that, and had it failed, we'd still be circling the moon. So I can assure you there were six eyeballs focused on those instruments." Bill Anders shared Borman's concern. "We knew we would be there forever if indeed that engine didn't work again," he later stated. "So that was a sobering thought." Back in mission control, George Low, the man who had convinced his NASA colleagues to change Apollo 8's mission from an Earth orbit to a historic journey to the moon, waited breathlessly to see if his bold decision would continue to be a success.

Approximately ninety hours into the mission, it was time for the final SPS burn. If it was successful, Apollo 8 would emerge from the moon's dark side and reestablish contact with Earth at nineteen minutes past midnight on Christmas Day, Houston time.

"We spent twenty hours going around the moon," Jim Lovell would later recount, "and were all kind of tired, and so we're programming the computer to turn on the engine . . . and on the computer comes up a little sign that says — a couple of numbers that essentially says, 'Are you really sure that you want to make this maneuver? This is your last chance to make a decision.' So I said, 'Frank, do we really want—?' Frank says, 'Push the button, push the button.'"

Lovell pushed the button and, for what he described as the "longest four minutes of my life," he waited as the SPS engine fired for a final time. For those in mission control, waiting to hear from the astronauts after that final burn was the most agonizing period of the flight. "We lost the signal . . . when they went behind the moon," Christopher Kraft said later, "and everybody, at that point, got up and started walking around in the room and I got on my intercom and said, 'Look, you guys, do what you want to do but I'm going to sit here and I want to pray a little bit and I'd like to have it quiet here because this is one hell of a tense moment for me and for those guys in the spacecraft.'"

At the scheduled moment, Ken Mattingly began attempting to reestablish contact with the spacecraft. "Apollo 8, Houston," he said into his microphone. Eighteen seconds later: "Apollo 8, Houston." Twenty seconds later: "Apollo 8, Houston." Fifty-two seconds later: "Apollo 8, Houston." Still there was no reply.

Then, just as the silence became unbearable, static was heard coming from Apollo 8. Then Jim Lovell's voice broke through. "Houston," he said, "Apollo 8. Over." "Hello, Apollo 8," Mattingly replied. "Loud and clear." "Please be informed," Lovell stated, "there is a Santa Claus." "That's affirmative," a greatly relieved Mattingly responded. "You are the best ones to know."

First up on the return agenda was another telecast. Once again, they began by aiming one of their cameras out one of the windows at the Earth. This time, it was not only to give those on Earth a view of themselves but also to show their home planet gradually getting larger as Apollo 8 headed back toward it. Then Borman described both the navigational system and the computer. Finally, Anders was shown eating a meal of chowder, chicken, orange juice, and cookies. It was one of the briefest of all the Apollo 8 telecasts, but arguably the most relaxed. As Borman would later say of their telecasts, "We all hammed it up a bit."

By now, they had been in space for more than four days and had spent nineteen hours orbiting the moon. Yet there were more challenges ahead of them. No other astronauts had ever plummeted from a quarter of a million miles at such a speed. No other astronauts had ever had so narrow a reentry target. Recalling the hair-raising experience, Anders said later, "We had to come 240,000 miles to hit something that was a reentry target about the size of a letter slot, seen from four miles away. We had to slide the letter into that slot."

"The last perils the Apollo 8 astronauts face," the *Washington Post* informed its readers, "are the hazards of reentry into the earth's atmosphere at the fastest speed man has ever traveled. Moving 24,630 miles an hour when it hits the earth's atmosphere . . . the Apollo spacecraft will be carrying the crew more than 7,000 miles an hour faster than any other space crew has ever experienced on reentry. If reentry is too steep, the spacecraft would decelerate too suddenly, and the force on Apollo would be more than 20 times the force of gravity, meaning the crew would be pressed by more than 20 times its own weight. Friction with the atmosphere at too steep a reentry would also heat the spacecraft beyond its design limits of 6,000 degrees. Just as bad a fate would befall the spacecraft if it struck the atmosphere at too shallow an angle. Like a flat stone skipping across water, it would bounce off the atmosphere and soar into a huge elliptical orbit around the earth."

The two days of homeward travel could have been routine, but two events—one a delightful surprise, the other a potentially disastrous mistake—marked that phase of the journey.

All three astronauts were celebrating Christmas. With all they had been through and all they had accomplished, it would have been a real treat for them to have something approximating a traditional holiday meal—especially given the bland, unappetizing food that had made up their menu since liftoff. They expected the same sort of freeze-dried meal for dinner, even on Christmas Day. To their amazement, when they opened that day's food locker, they found real turkey and real cranberry sauce wrapped with red and green ribbons. It was the best meal of their flight, and the surprise gift of fellow astronaut Deke Slayton. Slayton, in charge of NASA's astronaut office, had slipped three small bottles of brandy aboard to go with the special dinner. The ever-cautious Borman, however, decreed that they were to be left unopened. He was concerned that if the astronauts drank the brandy and anything went wrong during the rest of the flight, the press would blame it on alcohol consumption.

And something did go wrong. As Apollo 8 streaked toward Earth, Jim Lovell was checking his reentry data on the computer when he accidentally hit the wrong set of buttons and erased all the navigational information. Without the lost information, they wouldn't be able to enter the Earth's atmosphere at exactly the right angle. Luckily, Jim Lovell was a firm believer that "the real friends of the space voyager are the stars." Suddenly, despite all the most advanced technological equipment, the fate of Apollo 8 and its crew depended upon Lovell's ability to plot their reentry course by using a sextant to read the position of the stars. Not only did he manage it, it was later determined that Lovell's old-fashioned method of navigation had been every bit as accurate as the lost data. Later, commenting on how he had addressed a most serious issue, he stated, "Be thankful for problems. If they were less difficult, someone with less ability might have your job."

It was now Thursday, December 26, less than one day from reentry into the Earth's atmosphere. Anxious as they were, the crew of Apollo 8 had a final telecast to deliver. After giving viewers one last look at their planet from space, Bill Anders summed up their feelings when he stated, "As I look down on the earth here from so far out in space, I think I must have the feeling that the travelers in the old sailing ships used to have, going on a long voyage from home. And now that we're headed back, I have the feeling of being proud of the trip but still happy to be going home."

THE FAMILIES

As the crew of Apollo 8 made its long and hazardous way home, no one waited for them more anxiously than their families. Aside from the astronauts themselves, it was their wives who made the most enormous sacrifices on behalf of the mission. For weeks at a time, while Borman, Lovell, and Anders were in Florida training for their flight, their spouses remained in Houston, caring for their families and taking care of everything at home so that their husbands could concentrate totally on their vital mission. "I would say," recalled Marilyn Lovell, "[our husbands] were probably gone six days out of every week. We had to fend for ourselves, I mean, we didn't expect them to worry about us and I would say that we probably kept many things . . . to ourselves. As much as I tried to hide my fears even from myself it was not easy on any of us. And it was not easy on our children, especially the older children who understood what was happening."

The astronauts' wives faced another great challenge. "We were very much in the public eye and nobody had been trained for that," explained Valerie Anders. "We weren't trained for ticker-tape parades. Our children weren't trained for the public view that became part of their lives."

Frank Borman, Jim Lovell, and Bill Anders had all been both test pilots and fighter pilots, so their wives were accustomed to their husbands taking enormous risks and facing danger. But all three agreed that Apollo 8 was not just another test flight. They did, however, find a measure of comfort in the knowledge that their husbands, as military men, would have found themselves in a different type of perilous situation had they not been astronauts. "There were other wives . . . who were wives of fighter pilots, fighting in Vietnam," stated Valerie Anders, "and that's what our role would have been, had it not been this."

Like all the astronauts, Jim Lovell relied heavily on his family for support and encouragement. Here, he's being welcomed home from the Apollo 8 mission by (left to right) his daughters, Susan and Barbara; his wife, Marilyn; and his son Jay. The Lovells' youngest child, Jeffrey, was not woken up for the early-morning homecoming photo.

As they did before every flight, NASA officials installed a "squawk box" in each of the astronauts' homes. It allowed the families to listen in on the communication between Borman, Lovell, and Anders and mission control. And they didn't have to listen alone; as Valerie Anders explained, "Some of the astronauts would come [to the house] for each important phase of the mission so that if the wife had a question, they were there with their expertise to say, 'Well, you may hear this on the squawk box but this is what it means.'"

Above all else, the astronauts' wives were their husbands' greatest support, their greatest boosters, the ones who, more than anyone else, knew what made them tick and why they were doing what they did. Valerie Anders echoed the feelings of Marilyn Lovell and Susan Borman when she stated, "I knew my husband was skilled; I knew that he was a good pilot. I knew that he was competitive like all the others, and so I was cheering for him to be on a crew. And when that was achieved, I was really happy for him. And soon after he was selected for the crew of Apollo 8, the flight plan changed. And I did have some thoughts about this flight. . . . It was the first time man had been on the Saturn V [rocket]. It was the first time man had left their home planet to go out into space. It was the first time anybody went to the moon or behind the moon. And I knew the consequences of all those steps not working well. . . . I knew it was a Cold War tactic . . . and I knew that it was politically motivated. But when you're in it, and it's exciting, and . . . you just get carried away with that."

The telecast was barely over when the astronauts turned their full attention to reentry. They had spent hours rehearsing in the flight simulator, but none of them were truly prepared for the real thing. "Hang on!" Borman shouted as Apollo 8 entered the atmosphere and the gravitational pull on him and his crew rapidly mounted. Lovell was in charge of keeping track of the g's. "We're one g," he called out. Then some forty seconds later, "Five!" Another twenty seconds, "Six!" At this point, under six times the gravitational pull of someone standing on Earth, each astronaut weighed about half a ton.

The spacecraft's race through the atmosphere produced an almost unimaginable amount of friction, building up tremendous amounts of heat as it pushed against air molecules. The heat shield, designed to protect the spacecraft from burning up, began to glow, making the astronauts feel like they were, in Borman's words, "in a neon tube." Then the heat shield, as designed, began to melt, sending burning chunks flying past the spacecraft's window. "Pretty soon," Anders recalled, "it looked like we were inside a blowtorch."

Meanwhile, there was no possibility of radio contact between Apollo 8 and mission control. For the third time in less than four days, there was an agonizing period of silence, this time while controllers waited to hear that the astronauts had survived reentry. Once again a repeated call went out from mission control. "Apollo 8, come in. Apollo 8 . . . Apollo 8." Finally, Frank Borman's voice broke in. "Houston, Apollo 8. Over," he said. "It's looking good."

From its launch to its harrowing journey home, almost everything about Apollo 8 had been different from all other spaceflights. And that did not end with its splashdown. Like other American spaceflights, it came back to Earth over the ocean, giving its crew a softer touchdown than Soviet cosmonauts felt coming in on land, but no spaceflight had ever splashed down in the dark. It had been considered much too dangerous. Accordingly, when Apollo 8's revised

This photograph of Apollo 8's reentry was taken by a U.S. Air Force Airborne Lightweight Optical Tracking System camera mounted on a plane flying at forty thousand feet.

mission was charted, planners suggested a longer time in lunar orbit just so that they could splash down in daylight. But Borman voiced strong objections. "I didn't want to spend any more time in lunar orbit than absolutely necessary," he later explained. "Any prolonging of the mission simply increased the chances of something going wrong."

When officials argued back that a night landing not only increased the dangers of splashdown but also made recovery of the spacecraft and the astronauts within it much more risky, Borman had a ready answer. "What the hell does that matter?" he said. "If [something] doesn't work, we're all dead and it won't make any difference if anyone can see us."

As it turned out, Apollo 8's splashdown was not only unprecedented; it was remarkable. As the spacecraft's various parachutes deployed and slowed the craft down, mission controllers became alarmed for a never-before-experienced reason. As it slowed to about three hundred miles per hour and then to about 140, Apollo 8 was heading for its target area so accurately that it was in real danger of crashing directly into the USS *Yorktown,* the aircraft carrier waiting to recover it. Mission controllers were so concerned that they ordered the gigantic carrier to quickly change its position. Even so, Apollo 8 passed directly over the carrier and made splashdown less than three miles from where the huge vessel was now waiting.

At 4:51 a.m. local time on December 27, 1968, 147 hours after liftoff, Apollo 8 splashed down in the Pacific Ocean. It was a moment that would stay with all three astronauts forever. "We hit the water with a real bang!" Frank Borman later recalled. "I mean it was a big, big bang! And when we hit, we all got inundated with water. I don't know whether it came in one of the vents or whether it was just moisture that had collected on the environmental control system . . . Here were the three of us, having just come back from the moon, we're floating upside down in very rough seas—to me, rough seas."

A team of U.S. Navy swimmers prepares the Apollo 8 command module to be hoisted aboard the recovery ship, the USS *Yorktown*. Borman, Lovell, and Anders had already been taken safely aboard the vessel.

Bill Anders had his own recollection of the splashdown. "I can remember," he stated, "hanging from my straps with all the trash that had been collected on the floor, thinking, here we are, heroic lunar explorers, you know, hanging upside down in the ocean with all this dirt falling in our faces."

Confined in their bobbing capsule, the astronauts' joy in having splashed down safely was, of necessity, subdued. Those watching from around the country and particularly the people in the jam-packed mission control room in Houston, however, had no need for restraint. In mission control, there was a greater sense of relief and celebration than had welcomed home any previous mission. As soon as they knew Borman, Lovell, and Anders were safe, pandemonium broke out among those who had guided them from launch to splashdown, agonizing over their fates every step of the way. For some in the room, the realization of what they had accomplished was just beginning to sink in. "We grabbed for the lunar prize," declared an exultant Gene Kranz, "and we got it on our first shot."

Among the wildly cheering crowd was Michael Collins, the astronaut who had spent a week relaying messages from mission control to the crew. At that moment, his feelings could best be described as bittersweet. "For me personally," Collins would later write, "the moment was a conglomeration of emotions and memories. I was a basket case, emotionally wrung out. I had seen this flight evolve . . . in the interminable series of meetings at Houston . . . into an epic voyage. I had helped it grow. I had two years invested in it—it was my flight. Yet it was not my flight; I was but one of a hundred packed into a noisy room."

Because Borman had insisted on the night landing, the three astronauts had to remain in their capsule until dawn broke, waiting for it to be light enough that helicopters and swimmers—called frogmen—from the USS *Yorktown* could reach them. Apollo 8 had overturned when it splashed down, completely submerging the beacon designed to let the rescuers know just where it was in the vast, choppy Pacific waters. Luckily, even while hanging upside down from his harness, Borman had the presence of mind to hit the switch to inflate three large balloons that, within a few minutes, flipped the spacecraft into an upright position. With all the turbulence, Borman became very seasick and even threw up. Now that the flight was over and Borman was no longer commander, Naval Academy graduates Lovell and Anders couldn't resist affectionately making fun of the "West Point ground-pounder." Speaking later of their time bouncing on the waves, a good-natured Borman said he had to admit that Lovell and Anders "performed admirably after we were on the water, [and] the commander was taking a vacation."

Finally, it was light enough for the recovery operation to begin. As the recovery helicopter hovered over the spacecraft, someone yelled down to the only three humans who had ever been to the moon, "Is the moon made out of green cheese?" "No," Bill Anders replied without hesitation, "it's American cheese."

Borman recounted, "[Frogmen] jumped in and swam up and inflated various flotation devices to stabilize the spacecraft. And then using a special tool unlocked the hatch and I can remember this young frogman, Navy Seal, pulling the hatch back and poking his head in and then, with a shocked look kind of falling backwards. I didn't have time to contemplate that very much because we had to hop in the life raft which [was] now tied to the spacecraft and then hoisted by the helicopter onto the USS *Yorktown*. But later after we had been debriefed by the doctors and everybody, we had a chance to go out and look at the spacecraft and to meet the rescue crew," he continued. "So here was these Marines [and Navy Seals] all lined up, you know, in their uniforms and I recognized the young corporal there that had first stuck his head in. And I asked him; I said, 'Corporal, thanks a lot,' and you know, we hadn't shaved, you know, we were dirty, I said, 'We really must have looked bad,' and he said, without batting an eye, 'Sir, it wasn't how you looked; it was how you smelled.' And I did notice a very strange odor when I got out of the spacecraft and it turned out to be fresh air."

The Apollo 8 crew stands in the doorway of a recovery helicopter after arriving aboard the aircraft carrier USS *Yorktown*. Their capsule splashed down about one thousand miles southwest of Hawaii.

Thanks to television, millions of people around the world looked on as Frank Borman, Jim Lovell, and Bill Anders stepped out of the helicopter and onto the deck of the *Yorktown*. As they smiled and waved to the cameras, a proud realization on the part of millions of viewers around the globe set in. No one articulated it better than Marilyn Lovell. "Just to see them being taken out of the space capsule onto the ship . . . it was wonderful," she later stated. "I still remember how exciting it was to see these men, knowing where they'd been and what they'd done and how the country reacted. I don't think it impacted on me until they came back. . . . They really were heroes . . . and I never thought of it that way to start with, but they really were."

EPILOGUE

THERE HAD NEVER BEEN a mission like Apollo 8, which was evident in the praise the mission received almost from the moment its three astronauts were plucked out of the Pacific. "One of the historic moments in the development of the human race," proclaimed British royal astronomer Bernard Lovell. "The most fantastic story in all human history," declared Paris's *Journal du Dimanche*.

Although it was past two a.m., more than two thousand people gathered at Houston's Ellington Air Force Base on December 29 to greet the returned Apollo 8 astronauts, who are seen here standing at the microphones in the center of the crowd.

The formal celebrations of the historic achievement began on January 9, 1969, when Borman, Lovell, and Anders were paraded through Washington, DC, and addressed a special joint session of Congress. The next day, they flew to New York City, where the festivities included a giant parade in their honor and an address at the United Nations.

In the meantime, Apollo missions continued. On July 20, 1969, astronauts Neil Armstrong and Edwin "Buzz" Aldrin, as part of Apollo 11, fulfilled President Kennedy's vision by becoming the first humans to set foot on the moon. Armstrong's statement "That's one small step for a man, one giant leap for mankind" quickly became one of the most famous utterances in history.

In this photograph taken by Apollo 11 pilot Buzz Aldrin, astronaut Neil Armstrong, the first human to step on the moon, is seen standing next to the lunar module Eagle.

Geologist-astronaut Harrison Schmitt standing next to a boulder during the Apollo 17 moon landing. The Lunar Roving Vehicle is in the foreground.

A panoramic image taken during the Apollo 17 moon landing

Five more successful Apollo flights followed Apollo 11—and the "successful failure" of Apollo 13, which failed to land on the moon but saw all three of its astronauts safely home to Earth despite an onboard catastrophe—during which ten more Americans walked on the lunar surface. All of the lunar activities of the Apollo 17 astronauts were broadcast live and in color, but unlike the enormous audiences that tuned in for Apollo 8's Christmas broadcast, almost no one was watching. It would have been unimaginable only a few years earlier, but the public had lost interest in the space program. When Apollo 17 splashed down in the Pacific on December 19, 1972, crewed flights to the moon came to an end.

By the early 1970s, many felt that the billions of dollars being spent on space exploration would be better spent meeting the needs of people on Earth. Even before the first moon landing, Senator Edward Kennedy—President Kennedy's youngest brother—declared in May 1969 that money from the space program should be shifted into funding social programs to help the needy. Kennedy's sentiments were echoed by the *New Republic* magazine, which called for financial priority to be given to providing citizens with "decent housing, good schools, and a better life."

At the same time, the program had become a victim of its own success. "There was a real attitude . . . that, well, we've landed on the moon, so we've accomplished what we set out to do, so we don't have to spend any more money on space," wrote David Whalen, chairman of the space studies department at the University of North Dakota, Great Forks. Wernher von Braun put it more succinctly: "We have run out of Moons," he lamented.

As the space race waned, important, even startling, changes were taking place on Earth. By 1973, anti–Vietnam War sentiment in the United States had reached such a fever pitch that the government entered into a ceasefire agreement with North Vietnam. Two years later, South Vietnam fell to North Vietnamese forces and the war came to an end.

During the first half of the 1970s, friction between the United States and the Soviet Union eased considerably, resulting in a Cold War détente (a French word meaning release from tension). In 1975, the United States and the Soviet Union agreed to form an unlikely partnership to undertake the first international human spaceflight. Called the Apollo-Soyuz Test Project (ASTP), its three main purposes were to perfect systems that would allow Russian and American spacecraft to dock together, to provide the means for international space rescue, and to open the way for future joint American-Soviet human space flight.

NASA sent astronauts Deke Slayton, Tom Stafford, and Vance Brand to carry out the unprecedented mission in a spacecraft almost identical to Apollo 8's command module. For the Soviets, cosmonauts Aleksei Leonov and Valery Kubasov were blasted into orbit aboard a Soyuz craft, the Russian spacecraft that had been used for all cosmonaut flights since 1967. Proving that two different kinds of spacecraft from two different nations could successfully dock in space was the technical goal of the project, but the human side was equally important.

Before the launches, the two crews trained together. The joint experience exposed the astronauts and the cosmonauts to one another's hopes and dreams and started to break down cultural and language barriers. As Vance Brand explained, "We thought they were pretty aggressive people and . . . they probably thought we were monsters. So we very quickly broke through that, because when you deal with people that are in the same line of work as you are, and you're around them for a short time, why, you discover that, well, they're human beings."

The Apollo-Soyuz project took place between July 15 and July 24, 1975. On July 17 the two spacecraft docked in orbit 140 miles above the Earth. For the next two days, the American and Russian crews exchanged visits and conducted five joint experiments.

In NASA's report on the joint mission, the American space administration stated that "the flight was more a symbol of the lessening of tensions between the two superpowers than a significant scientific endeavor, a sharp contrast with

In preparation for the historic Apollo-Soyuz
project, American astronaut Thomas Stafford
(left), joined here by veteran Russian cosmonaut Andriyan Nikolaev (right), spent time in
the Soviets' flight simulator.

the competition for international prestige that had fueled much of the space activities of both nations since the late 1950s."

In 1985, a reformer became the leader of the Soviet Union. Unlike his predecessors, Mikhail Gorbachev was intent on reforming the sluggish Soviet economy. In 1986, he introduced policies that allowed a number of Western ideas and products into the Soviet Union, policies that also granted newfound freedoms of assembly, speech, and religion to Soviet citizens.

They were bold moves, and Gorbachev himself failed to understand that granting these freedoms after years of extreme oppression would only make his people yearn for even more freedoms. In June 1989, the people of Poland elected a noncommunist government. Inspired by this act of revolt and Gorbachev's refusal to act militarily against it, other Eastern European communist regimes fell, one after another. In the fall of 1989, East and West Germans tore down the Berlin Wall — long a symbol of the Cold War — with sledgehammers and pickaxes. Communist governments in Czechoslovakia and Hungary were overthrown, while the formerly communist Baltic states of Estonia, Latvia, and Lithuania declared their independence.

For the Soviet Union, the worst was still to come. In December 1991, the three nations at the heart of the USSR — Ukraine, Belarus, and Russia itself — declared their independence. The Soviet Union had collapsed. The Cold War was over.

Immediately after the Apollo 8 mission ended, Frank Borman was sent on a goodwill tour of eight Western European countries by President Richard Nixon. In London, Borman met the queen and the British prime minister, gave a major speech to the Royal Society, and sat in the public gallery of the House of Commons while one member of Parliament after another hailed what he, Lovell, and Anders had done as one of the greatest achievements in history.

In Germany, Borman met with Hermann Oberth, the father of German rocketry, and spoke to an audience of Germany's leading space scientists, where he declared, "We are first and foremost not Germans or Russians or Americans but earthmen." In July 1969, he became the first American to visit Star City, the Russian counterpart to NASA's Manned Spacecraft Center in Houston. This, more than the grandeur of the Houses of Parliament or the historical significance of Hermann Oberth, struck those hoping for cooperation in space between the world's two great powers as Borman's most important visit of all. For millions, it was one of the first signs that the space war was indeed over.

The American Apollo project and the Soviet Soyuz project grew out of the Cold War's rivalries but developed into the joint Apollo-Soyuz project. Today, the cooperative spirit of Apollo-Soyuz lives on in a much larger way: the International Space Station (ISS). A major endeavor in space architecture, the ISS is a project of not just NASA and Russia's Roscosmos, but also the Japan Aerospace Exploration Agency (JAXA), the European Space Agency (ESA), and the Canadian Space Agency (CSA). Assembly began in November 1998, and the space station has been continuously lived in since American Bill Shepherd and Russians Sergei Krikalev and Yuri Gidzenko became its first residents on November 2, 2000. Crewmembers conduct studies in onboard laboratories that could not be carried out anywhere else. Their research not only paves the way for human missions that will reach farther into space than ever before but also informs the science and technology that shapes life on Earth.

And all these achievements trace back to Apollo 8's accomplishment. As the *Christian Science Monitor* stated at the time, "No man, no nation, no race can fail to think more broadly as a result of men's having circled the Moon. With such an achievement in their eyes, fewer persons will be tempted to believe that Earth's problems, however stark, are beyond settlement. . . . The space program's greatest and healthiest impact is almost certain to be on events back here on Earth."

The International Space Station, backdropped by Earth and a cloud-dotted sky, as seen by the space shuttle *Discovery*

LIFE AFTER APOLLO 8

When he introduced Apollo 8's crew to the assembled United Nations delegates, Secretary General U Thant stated, "These three pioneering heroes of space have seen both the moon and the earth as no other men have ever seen them. Thanks to their inspiring adventure we, the earth people, all henceforth will enjoy a new perspective of the universe and earth's position in it, and an entirely new and immensely broadened dimension with regard to distance and space. I am very happy to introduce these three pathfinders in space, the first true universalists."

Thant was right. Having seen the Earth as no other humans had ever seen it, the three Apollo 8 astronauts had a unique understanding of the fact that we were indeed all "riders on the Earth together."

FRANK BORMAN

After retiring from the air force with the rank of colonel, Frank Borman became a member of the board of directors of several major corporations and organizations, including Home Depot and the National Geographic Society. He also began what would be a long relationship with Eastern Airlines, serving from 1976 to 1986 as the company's chief executive officer and chairman of the board.

JIM LOVELL

Almost as soon as the Apollo 8 flight ended, Jim Lovell, having already spent more time in space than any other human being, began training as part of the backup crew for Apollo 11. It wasn't until April 11, 1970, that he lifted off again, this time as commander of Apollo 13. Its mission included landing on the moon, exploring it further, and collecting soil and rock samples, but its moon landing was abandoned after the oxygen system on board exploded. Lovell was awarded a Congressional Space Medal of Honor for his part in saving the lives of his fellow Apollo 13 crewmembers, but he never returned to space—or the moon. Much to his disappointment, he remains the only human ever to have twice circled the moon without stepping foot on it.

BILL ANDERS

Like Jim Lovell, Bill Anders began his post–Apollo 8 career as part of the Apollo 11 backup crew. He then retired from NASA but continued to work for the government, serving as executive secretary for the National Aeronautics and Space Council, as head commissioner for all nuclear and non-nuclear power research and development on the five-member Atomic Energy Commission, as chairman of the newly established Nuclear Regulatory Commission (NRC), and, finally, as United States ambassador to Norway.

In 1977, Anders ended twenty-six years of government service and entered the business world, eventually serving as vice president and general manager of General Electric, senior executive vice president of Textron, and chief executive officer and chairman of the board of General Dynamics.

Asked what thrilled him most about the Apollo 8 mission, Anders replied that it "represented a massive opportunity to explore. . . . It was not so much the flying or the patriotism. Those were big elements but the main thing was exploration. . . . I really hoped, not only to be able to go to the moon, but be able to walk on it someday. At least I got fifty percent of that."

SOURCE NOTES

PROLOGUE

p. 1: "I believe that this nation . . . put him there": quoted in Cadbury, p. 246.

p. 6: "In the eyes of the world . . . second in everything": quoted in DeGroot, p. 72.

p. 6: "People of the whole world . . . has been beaten": quoted in Zimmerman, p. 53.

p. 6: "only Presidential emphasis . . . to the stars" and "How can we catch up? . . . more important": quoted in Cadbury, p. 243.

CHAPTER 1: A HISTORIC CHANGE IN PLANS

p. 11: "Everything about the Saturn V . . . a forklift truck": quoted in Cadbury, p. 311

p. 14: "If there is a small rocket . . . speeds are added": quoted in "Hermann J. Oberth," International Space Hall of Fame, New Mexico Museum of Space History, http://www.nmspacemuseum.org/halloffame/index.php?type=name.

p. 14: "It is difficult to say . . . reality of tomorrow": quoted in "Dr. Robert H. Goddard, American Rocketry Pioneer," Goddard Space Flight Center, NASA, https://www.nasa.gov/centers/goddard/about/history/dr_goddard.html.

p. 17: "We learned . . . gotten there first": quoted in Polkow.

p. 17: "Low very quietly . . . for that mission": *Race to the Moon.*

p. 17: "NASA wanted to beat . . . engineering goal": ibid.

pp. 17–20: "Can we do a lunar . . . difficult thing to do": ibid.

p. 20: "For the people . . . about your own": quoted in Brice.

p. 20: "I was ecstatic . . . something going wrong": "To the Moon," Transcript.

p. 20: "Are you out of your *mind*?": quoted in Chaikin, *Man on the Moon,* p. 58.

p. 23: "In every century . . . dream of mankind": quoted in Cadbury, p. 129.

CHAPTER 2: AGAINST ALL ODDS

pp. 31–32: "We shifted into . . . navigational updates": Borman, Lovell, and Anders, p. 29.

p. 32: "I spent eighteen . . . for any malfunction": ibid., p. 30.

p. 34: "I didn't go into the NASA . . . [moon] rocks": *Race to the Moon.*

p. 35: "What's the main objective? . . . Why complicate it?": quoted in Evans, "'Launch Commit.'"

p. 35: "I don't know that I could spend . . . with Lovell, though": *Race to the Moon.*

p. 40: "The Saturn V was such . . . Wonderment": quoted in Chaikin, *Voices,* p. 20.

p. 40: "threading the needle . . . million miles away": Kranz, p. 240.

p. 40: "This will be the first . . . three painful days": *Washington Post,* December 21, 1968, *Race to the Moon.*

p. 41: "During our preflight . . . first lunar flight": Borman, Lovell, and Anders, p. 30.

p. 41: "I gave some thought . . . not coming back": quoted in Kluger.

p. 41: "If you worried . . . the first place": ibid.

p. 43: "Fire! We've got a fire in the cockpit": quoted in Cadbury, p. 303.

p. 44 "Get us out. . . . We're burning up!": ibid.

p. 44: "If we die . . . risk of life": quoted in Barbour, p. 125.

p. 45: "We knew that the Russians . . . first time. Everything": *Race to the Moon.*

p. 45: "She's building . . . to build it!": quoted in Evans, " 'Launch Commit.' "

p. 45: "awesome . . . Empire State Building taking off": quoted in Poole, p. 19.

p. 45: "ten times more . . . way to Paris": quoted in Zimmerman, p. 11.

p. 47: "slowly, as in . . . fire and smoke" and "The Earth shakes . . . prolonged": Anne Morrow Lindbergh, "The Heron and the Astronaut," *Life,* February 28, 1969, p. 22.

p. 47: "It was all there . . . rested in that spaceship": *Race to the Moon.*

p. 48: "the guiding-star of my life": quoted in "Short Biography," Hermann Oberth Raumfahrt Museum website, http://www.oberth-museum.org/index_e.html.

p. 51: Recent revelations underscore . . . work on the V-2s: Cadbury, pp. 335–339.

p. 51: "The greatest rocket scientist in history": Robin Williams, "Wernher von Braun, (1912–1977)" NASA Earth Observatory website, May 2, 2001, https://earthobservatory.nasa.gov/Features/vonBraun/vonbraun.php.

CHAPTER 3: TO THE MOON

p. 55: "There was a startling . . . hadn't simulated": quoted in Chaikin, *Voices,* p. 20.

p. 55: "were thrown forward . . . into the seat": quoted in Evans, " 'Launch Commit.' "

pp. 55–57: "Instinctively, I threw . . . rookies on that one": *Race to the Moon.*

p. 56: "After insertion . . . the whole tour": Borman, Lovell, and Anders, p. 30.

p. 56: "In the early stages . . . had ever been before": ibid., p. 29.

p. 56: "Tell Conrad he lost his record": quoted in Cortright, chapter 9.5.

p. 56: "Tell the people in Tierra . . . is out there": Woods and O'Brien, "Apollo 8: Day 1: The Green Team and Separation," https://history.nasa.gov/afj/ap08fj/03day1_green_sep.html.

p. 58: "All of us had flown . . . *what God sees*": quoted in Poole, p. 20.

p. 59: "I think one of the biggest . . . some hard tradeoffs": quoted in Slagle.

p. 59: "Apollo 8, you are go for TLI": quoted in Zimmerman, p. 17.

p. 59: "I can remember . . . our technical jargon": Michael Collins, NASA Johnson Space Center Oral History Project, October 8, 1997, https://www.jsc.nasa.gov/history/oral_histories/CollinsM/CollinsM_10-8-97.htm.

p. 62: "You're on your way. You're *really* on your way!": quoted in Zimmerman, pp. 17–18.

p. 62: "When I heard the crew . . . I was crying": Kranz, p. 242.

p. 62: "we sweated the burn . . . belong to the moon forever": Borman, Lovell, and Anders, p. 29.

p. 63: "The moon is moving along . . . room for error": *Race to the Moon.*

p. 63: "It was a delicate . . . Earth for eternity": quoted in "Frank Borman," International Space Hall of Fame, New Mexico Museum of Space History, http://www.nmspacemuseum.org/halloffame/index.php?type=name.

p. 63: "I did something . . . only reluctantly": Borman, Lovell, and Anders, p. 28.

p. 64: "The moon appears . . . fairest planets": quoted in Zimmerman, p. 152.

p. 66: "This transmission is coming . . . in zero g": Woods and O'Brien, "Apollo 8: Day 2: The Maroon Team," https://history.nasa.gov/afj/ap08fj/07day2_maroon.html.

p. 68: "I certainly wish we could . . . covers of white clouds": quoted in Zimmerman, p. 76.

p. 68: "let everyone see . . . the beard race": ibid.

p. 68: "I said 'no' a lot . . . NASA was right": *Race to the Moon.*

p. 69: "What I keep imagining . . . part of the Earth": Woods and O'Brien, "Apollo 8: Day 3: The Green Team," https://history.nasa.gov/afj/ap08fj/09day3_green.html.

p. 69: "You better hope . . . the blue part": ibid.

CHAPTER 4: A WHOLE NEW WORLD

pp. 72–73: "We had a loss of signal . . . take a break'": *Race to the Moon.*

p. 73: "It occurred to me . . . of a different body]": Borman, Lovell, and Anders, p. 30.

p. 73: "Suddenly, we saw millions . . . a little bit": *Race to the Moon.*

p. 73: "On the computer . . . sixty miles below": ibid.

pp. 73–74: "We were like three school kids . . . really amazing sight": "To the Moon," Transcript.

p. 74: "I had developed a mind's-eye . . . ever-decreasing diameter": Borman, Lovell, and Anders, p. 30.

p. 76: "What I saw flashing . . . the lead wagon": ibid.

p. 76: "We got it! . . . in lunar orbit": quoted in Evans, "'Launch Commit.'"

p. 76: "When we heard from the crew . . . in lunar orbit!": *Race to the Moon.*

p. 76: "Everyone grew silent for a minute": quoted in Cadbury, p. 320.

p. 77: "It was Christmas Eve . . . at this moment'": *Race to the Moon.*

p. 77: "Well, did you guys . . . the moon?" and "Just hope . . . on New Year's": quoted in Zimmerman, p. 117.

p. 78: "Thousands of people made this possible": quoted in "Apollo 8 Man Around the Moon," NASA EP-66, Office of Public Affairs, NASA, https://er.jsc.nasa.gov/seh/apollo8.html.

p. 78: "The Apollo 8 crew . . . contractor network": *Race to the Moon.*

p. 78: "I can remember going through . . . do our job'": quoted in McKie.

p. 79: "Chris Kraft . . . ran it with compassion": *Race to the Moon.*

p. 79: "like a cherished . . . we should do?'": ibid.

p. 79: "We call the first row . . . a proud bunch": ibid.

CHAPTER 5: EARTHRISE

p. 81: "Oh, my God! . . . is that pretty": quoted in Zimmerman, p. 199.

p. 83: "We were trained . . . above that horizon": quoted in Scott Neuman, "On Anniversary of Apollo 8, How the 'Earthrise' Photo Was Made," *Morning Edition,* NPR, December 23, 2013, http://www.npr.org/sections /thetwo-way/2013/12/23/256605845/on-anniversary-of-apollo-8-how-the-earthrise-photo-was-made.

p. 83: "Hey, don't . . . it's not scheduled": quoted in Zimmerman, p. 199.

p. 83: "C'mon, hurry up . . . have much time": *Race to the Moon.*

p. 83: "Wait a minute . . . Calm down, Lovell": NASA, Apollo 8 Onboard Voice Transcription, p. 114, https://www.jsc.nasa .gov/history/mission_trans/AS08_CM.PDF.

p. 83: "forever change . . . planet and ourselves": Drew Dellinger, "Christmas 1968 and the Photograph That Changed the World," *Drew Dellinger* (blog), December 25, 2008, http://drewdellinger.org/pages/blog /138/christmas-1968-and-the-p.

pp. 83–86: "The view of the earth . . . really is 'one world' ": Borman, Lovell, and Anders, p. 29.

p. 86: "when I looked up . . . home planet, the Earth": quoted in Poole, p. 2.

p. 86: "We came around . . . in the universe": *Race to the Moon.*

p. 86: "Once a photograph . . . be let loose": quoted in Redfern.

p. 87: "Look again at that dot . . . in a sunbeam": Sagan, p. 6.

p. 87: "I think that picture . . . on everybody": *Race to the Moon.*

pp. 87–88: "For the first time . . . are truly brothers": quoted in Poole, p. 8.

p. 88: "Our planet is . . . from ourselves": Sagan, p. 7.

p. 88: "We should cherish . . . from the Moon": quoted in Poole, p. 8.

p. 88 "How can you look . . . pale blue dot": quoted in Caroline Sheffield, "Why Do We Go to Outer Space?" Virgin Galactic website, February 3, 2014, https://www.virgin.com/virgin-unite/leadership-and-advocacy/why-do-we-go-outer-space.

p. 88: "Looking back . . . for the Earth": Poole, p. 8.

pp. 88–89: "I date my own reawakening . . . we still can": quoted in Poole, p. 9.

p. 89: "I thought it would be . . . of the mission": quoted in Kluger.

p. 91: "Slowly, over the misty . . . upon the nation": Alexander Gardner, *Gardner's Photographic Sketchbook of the Civil War* (1866; reprint, New York: Dover, 1959), caption to plate 36.

p. 92: "Their roots were . . . their spirit": quoted in Milton Meltzer, *Dorothea Lange: A Photographer's Life* (Syracuse, NY: Syracuse University Press, 2000), p. 97.

p. 92: "I did not ask her name . . . helped me": "Migrant Mother, 1936," *Eyewitness to History,* http://www.eyewitnesstohistory .com/migrantmother.htm.

CHAPTER 6: AN EXTRAORDINARY BROADCAST

p. 97: "I'll stay up . . . get some rest": quoted in Chaikin, *Man on the Moon,* p. 117.

p. 97: "No. You try . . . make another mistake": ibid.

p. 97: "I want you . . . Right now!": ibid.

pp. 97–99: "This is Apollo 8 . . . place to live or work": quoted in Zimmerman, pp. 241–242.

p. 99: "I think the best way . . . vastness of space": ibid., p. 243.

p. 99: "I think the thing that impressed . . . of the terrain": ibid., pp. 242–243.

p. 99: "The sky up here . . . inch is pockmarked": ibid., p. 243.

p. 99: "How finite the Earth . . . mote in infinity": *Race to the Moon.*

p. 99: "The thing about Apollo . . . their home planet": ibid.

p. 103: "We figure . . . man in history": quoted in Zimmerman, p. 230.

p. 103: "It was too flippant. It did not match the event": ibid., p. 232.

p. 104: "a significant statement . . . event of exploration": *Race to the Moon.*

p. 104: "Why don't they . . . book of Genesis?": ibid.

p. 104: "You couldn't ask . . . world's religions": quoted in Zimmerman, p. 237.

p. 104: "We are now approaching . . . send to you": quoted in Chaikin, *Man on the Moon,* p. 121.

pp. 104–106: "the most profound . . . the human race": Zimmerman, p. xi.

p. 106: "'In the beginning . . . the darkness'": quoted in Chaikin, *Man on the Moon,* p. 121.

p. 106: "'And God called the light . . . the second day'": ibid., p. 122.

p. 106: "'And God said . . . the good Earth:'" ibid.

p. 106: "For those moments . . . on my cheeks": Kranz, p. 246.

p. 106: "I've never seen this place . . . the perfect time": *Race to the Moon.*

pp. 106–107: "You know, I'm afraid . . . the right thing": ibid.

p. 107: "To me . . . if you will": quoted in Chaikin, *Voices,* p. 45.

p. 108: "the most hated woman in America": Jane Howard, "'The Most Hated Woman in America,'" *Life,* June 19, 1964, p. 91.

CHAPTER 7: RETURN TO EARTH

p. 113: "I think the premier . . . focused on those instruments": "To the Moon," Transcript.

p. 113: "We knew we would be . . . sobering thought": ibid.

pp. 113–114: "We spent twenty hours . . . push the button'": ibid.

p. 114: "longest four minutes of my life": ibid.

p. 114: "We lost the signal . . . guys in the spacecraft": *Race to the Moon.*

p. 114: "Apollo 8, Houston . . . Apollo 8, Houston": quoted in Zimmerman, p. 253.

p. 114: "Houston, Apollo 8. Over. . . . best ones to know": quoted in Chaikin, *Man on the Moon,* p. 126.

p. 114: "We all hammed it up a bit": *Race to the Moon.*

p. 115: "We had to come 240,000 . . . into that slot": "To the Moon," Transcript.

p. 115: "The last perils . . . around the earth": *Washington Post,* December 28, 1968, quoted in *Race to the Moon.*

p. 116: "the real friends . . . are the stars": quoted in "James A. Lovell Jr.," International Space Hall of Fame, New Mexico Museum of Space History, http://www.nmspacemuseum.org/halloffame/index.php?type=name.

p. 116: "Be thankful for . . . have your job": ibid.

p. 116: "As I look down on the earth . . . be going home": quoted in Zimmerman, p. 263.

p. 117: "I would say . . . what was happening": *Race to the Moon.*

p. 117: "We were very much . . . part of their lives": ibid.

p. 118: "There were other wives . . . not been this": ibid.

p. 119: "Some of the astronauts . . . what it means,": ibid.

p. 119: "I knew my husband . . . carried away with that": ibid.

p. 120: "Hang on!," "We're one g," "Five!," and "Six!": quoted in Zimmerman, pp. 267–268.

p. 120: "in a neon tube": ibid, p. 268.

p. 120: "Pretty soon . . . inside a blowtorch": *Race to the Moon.*

p. 120: "Apollo 8, come in. . . . Apollo 8": quoted in Cadbury, p. 320.

p. 120: "Houston, Apollo 8. . . . looking good": Woods and O'Brien, "Apollo 8: Day 6: The Maroon Team — Splashdown."

p. 122: "I didn't want to spend . . . something going wrong": quoted in Zimmerman, p. 266.

p. 122: "What the hell . . . anyone can see us": ibid.

p. 122: "We hit the water . . . to me, rough seas": *Race to the Moon.*

p. 124: "I can remember hanging . . . in our faces": ibid.

p. 124: "We grabbed for the lunar. . . our first shot": Kranz, p. 246.

p. 124: "For me personally . . . a noisy room": quoted in Evans, " 'Launch Commit.' "

p. 125 "West Point ground-pounder" and "performed admirably . . . taking a vacation": quoted in Zimmerman, pp. 269–270.

p. 125: "Is the moon made out of green cheese?" and "No, it's American cheese": "To the Moon," Transcript.

p. 125: "[Frogmen] jumped in . . . turned out to be fresh air": *Race to the Moon.*

p. 127: "Just to see them . . . they really were": ibid.

EPILOGUE

p. 129: "One of the historic . . . the human race": *Race to the Moon.*

p. 129: "the most fantastic . . . all human history:" ibid.

p. 132: "That's one small . . . leap for mankind": quoted in Cadbury, p. 233.

p. 134: "decent housing . . . a better life": quoted in Zimmerman, p. 280.

p. 134: "There was a real attitude . . . money on space": quoted in Brice.

p. 134: "We have run out of Moons": "The Great Space Race: How the U.S. Beat the Russians to the Moon," *Life,* September 30, 2016.

p. 135: "We thought they were . . . human beings": quoted in "An Orbiting Partnership Is Born," NASA News and Features Archives, July 15, 2005, https://www.nasa.gov/vision/space/features/astp_30.html.

pp. 135–137: "the flight was . . . the late 1950s": Roger Launius, Colin Fries, and Abe Gibson, "Defining Events in NASA History, 1958–2006," NASA, https://history.nasa.gov/printFriendly/Defining-chron.htm.

p. 138: "We are first and foremost . . . earthmen": quoted in Zimmerman, p. 288.

p. 138: "No man, no nation . . . here on Earth": quoted in Poole, p. 7.

LIFE AFTER APOLLO 8

p. 140: "These three pioneering . . . true universalists": U Thant, "Astronauts - Apollo 8 - welcoming statement, 10 January 1969," United Nations Archives, S-0885-0001-11-00001.

p. 144: "represented a massive . . . percent of that": *Race to the Moon.*

BIBLIOGRAPHY

Barbour, John. *Footprints on the Moon*. New York: Associated Press, 1969.

Borman, Frank. *Countdown: An Autobiography*. New York: Silver Arrow, 1988.

———, James Lovell, and Bill Anders. "The Astronauts Write Their Stories of the Flight." *Life,* January 17, 1969, pp. 26–31.

Brice, Arthur. "Apollo 8 Astronauts Remember Historic Voyage." CNN Online, December 22, 2008. http://edition.cnn .com/2008/TECH/space/12/22/apollo8.anniversary/index.html.

Cadbury, Deborah. *Space Race: The Epic Battle Between America and the Soviet Union for Dominion of Space*. New York: HarperCollins, 2006.

Chaikin, Andrew. *A Man on the Moon: The Voyages of the Apollo Astronauts*. New York: Penguin, 2007.

———. *Voices from the Moon: Apollo Astronauts Describe Their Lunar Experiences*. New York: Viking Studio, 2009.

Collins, Michael. *Liftoff: The Story of America's Adventure in Space*. New York: Grove, 1988.

Cortright, Edgar M., ed. *Apollo Expeditions to the Moon*. Washington, DC: NASA History Office, 2006. https://history.nasa .gov/SP-350/cover.html.

DeGroot, Gerard. *Dark Side of the Moon: The Magnificent Madness of the American Lunar Ques*t. New York: New York University Press, 2006.

Evans, Ben. " 'Launch Commit': The Voyage of Apollo 8 (Part 1)." AmericaSpace website, December 20, 2014. http://www .americaspace.com/2014/12/20/launch-commit-the-voyage-of-apollo-8-part-1/.

———. " 'There Is a Santa Claus': The Voyage of Apollo 8 (Part 2)." AmericaSpace website, December 21, 2014. http://www .americaspace.com/2014/12/21/there-is-a-santa-claus-the-voyage-of-apollo-8-part-2/.

Harford, James. *Korolev: How One Man Masterminded the Soviet Drive to Beat America to the Moon*. New York: Wiley, 1997.

Howland, Stan. "What the Apollo's Men Saw on the Moon." *Sydney Morning Herald,* December 26, 1968.

Khrushchev, Nikita. *Khrushchev Remembers*. Boston: Little, Brown, 1970.

Kluger, Jeffrey. "Remembering Apollo 8, Man's First Trip to the Moon." *Time,* December 24, 2013. http://content.time.com /time/nation/article/0,8599,1868461,00.html.

Kraft, Chris. *Flight: My Life in Mission Control.* New York: Dutton, 2001.

Kranz, Gene. *Failure Is Not an Option: Mission Control from Mercury to Apollo 13 and Beyond.* New York: Simon & Schuster, 2000.

McKie, Robin. "The Mission That Changed Everything." *The Guardian,* November 29, 2008. https://www.theguardian.com /science/2008/nov/30/apollo-8-mission.

New York Times Staff. *Apollo 8: The Dramatic Story of Man's Greatest Adventure.* New York: New York Times Books, 1969.

Polkow, Dennis. "How Apollo 8 Gave a Beleaguered Nation a Christmas Gift." *Chicago Tribune,* December 24, 1998. http://articles.chicagotribune.com/1998-12-24/features/9812240262_1_apollo-astronauts-moon.

Poole, Robert. *Earthrise: How Man First Saw the Earth.* New Haven: Yale University Press, 2008.

Race to the Moon: The Daring Adventure of Apollo 8. PBS Home Video, *American Experience,* 2005. DVD.

Redfern, Martin. "A New View of Home." *The Independent,* April 20, 1996. http://www.independent.co.uk/arts -entertainment/science-a-new-view-of-home-1306095.html.

Sagan, Carl. *Pale Blue Dot: A Vision of the Human Future in Space.* New York: Ballantine, 1997.

Shepard, Alan, and Deke Slayton. *Moon Shot: The Inside Story of America's Race to the Moon.* Nashville: Turner, 1994.

Slagle, Alton. "Apollo 8, the First Manned Mission to the Moon." *New York Daily News,* December 22, 1968. http://www .nydailynews.com/news/national/apollo-8-launches-moon-1968-article-1.2473201.

"To the Moon." *NOVA.* PBS. July 13, 1999. http://www.pbs.org/wgbh/nova/tothemoon/. Transcript, http://www.pbs.org /wgbh/nova/transcripts/2610tothemoon.html.

Wolfe, Tom. *The Right Stuff.* New York: Farrar, Straus & Giroux, 1979.

Woods, David, and Frank O'Brien, eds. *Apollo 8 Flight Journal.* NASA History Division. April 10, 2017. https://history.nasa .gov/afj/ap08fj/index.html.

Young, John. *America, Russia, and the Cold War, 1941–1998.* New York: Longman, 1999.

Zimmerman, Robert. *Genesis: The Story of Apollo 8.* New York: Dell, 1998.

INDEX

Page numbers in italics indicate images or captions.

ACKNOWLEDGMENTS

I am most grateful to Rachel Eeva Wood for the marvelous interior design and to Matt Roeser for the extraordinary jacket and cover. And I owe a huge debt of gratitude to Hannah Mahoney for the meticulous way every fact and quotation was checked and authenticated. Thanks also to Emily Quinan, Rebecca Demont, Linda Rizkalla, and Carol Sandler for their much appreciated help. Once again, I am indebted to Miriam Newman for her valuable insights and contributions. And finally, and as always, there are not words adequate enough to express what I owe Hilary Van Dusen for the way she shaped this book and guided its author. Thanks, Hilary, for sharing the telling of this amazing story with me.